Alastair Duncan
was for fourteen years associated with
Christie's, New York, latterly as the Consultant for Nineteenth- and
Twentieth-Century Decorative Arts. After joining the auction
house in 1977, he organized and catalogued a great number of sales
devoted to Art Nouveau and Art Deco and nineteenth-century
decorative arts. He has acted as guest curator for exhibitions at the
Smithsonian Institution, Washington, D.C., and is now an indepen-
dent consultant specializing in the decorative arts of the nineteenth
and twentieth centuries. He is the author of many books, including
Art Deco Furniture, *Art Nouveau Furniture*, *Art Nouveau and Art Deco
Lighting*, *Glass by Gallé*, *American Art Deco*, *Louis Majorelle* and
Masterworks of Louis Comfort Tiffany, all published by Thames and
Hudson, and has contributed articles to journals such as
Vogue and *Connoisseur*.

WORLD OF ART

This famous series
provides the widest available
range of illustrated books on art in all its aspects.
If you would like to receive a complete list
of titles in print please write to:
THAMES AND HUDSON
30 Bloomsbury Street, London WC1B 3QP
In the United States please write to:
THAMES AND HUDSON INC.
500 Fifth Avenue, New York, New York 10110

Printed in Singapore

ALASTAIR DUNCAN

Art Nouveau

170 illustrations, 32 in color

THAMES AND HUDSON

Special acknowledgments to MaryBeth McCaffrey

Designed by Liz Rudderham

Any copy of this book issued by the publisher
as a paperback is sold subject to the condition
that it shall not by way of trade or otherwise
be lent, resold, hired out or otherwise circulated
without the publisher's prior consent
in any form of binding or cover other than that in
which it is published and without a similar
condition including these words being imposed
on a subsequent purchaser.

© 1994 Thames and Hudson Ltd, London

First published in the United States of America in 1994 by
Thames and Hudson Inc., 500 Fifth Avenue,
New York, New York 10110

Library of Congress Catalog Card Number 93-61372

ISBN 0-500-20273-7

All Rights Reserved. No part of this publication
may be reproduced or transmitted in any form or
by any means, electronic or mechanical, including
photocopy, recording or any other information
storage and retrieval system, without prior permission
in writing from the publisher.

Printed and bound in Singapore

Contents

CHAPTER ONE

Introduction

It is best stated at the outset: *Art Nouveau was a movement, not a style,* one that evolved differently in different countries in the late 19th century, with the single purpose of defeating the established order within the applied and fine arts. Without an understanding of this fact, it would be impossible to reconcile the many disparate modern styles that emerged at the time under a single label. How else, for example, could the linear austerity of Charles Rennie Mackintosh share a common heritage and goal with the hothouse sinuosities of Victor Horta and Hector Guimard? Or the chequerboard geometry of Josef Hoffmann and Koloman Moser bear comparison with the floral profusions of Emile Gallé and Louis Majorelle? And how could any of these logically be compared to the designs of the isolated Catalan, Antoni Gaudí?

No single architect or artist-designer or school epitomized the 'New Art'; each sought to settle his account with historicism in his own way. The response was exuberant on the banks of the Seine and the Rhine, and serious and restrained in Glasgow and Vienna. Nor did its exponents embrace it with equal enthusiasm and success, or for an equal amount of time. The French art historian, Maurice Rheims, aptly compared the Art Nouveau movement to a rocket: some of its participants chose to drop out soon after it had been launched; others at the apex of its trajectory; others, again, stayed until the very end, after it had peaked and dissolved into myriad fragments. All were in revolt against a century of mediocrity and pastiche, yet each was free to express his opposition as he chose. This was evident as early as 1902, when the critic A. D. F. Hamlin wrote, in an analysis of the fledgling Art Nouveau movement in the United States, that there was little agreement among its adherents beyond 'an underlying character of protest against the traditional and the commonplace.'

Resistance to the Victorian cult of revivalism had emerged well before the turn of the century. As early as 1836, Alfred de Musset wrote in *Confession d'un Enfant du Siècle*, 'The apartments of the rich are cabinets of curiosities: a conglomeration of Classical Antiquity, Gothic, Renaissance, Louis XIII . . . something from every century except our own, a predicament which has arisen in no other period . . . so that we seem to be subsisting on the ruins of the past, as if the end of the world were near.'

The Crystal Palace exhibition of 1851 in London revealed that matters had by then further regressed, due to the Industrial Revolution and the advent of the machine, which could now manufacture an avalanche of period cast-offs to meet the decorating whims of the upper classes and an expanding bourgeoisie.

The average 19th-century interior was solemn and tedious, with little air and less light. Every conceivable surface and space was used to create the dissonant and fusty mix of furniture, bric-à-brac, wall hangings and textiles that came to characterize home-ownership in the Victorian age. Matters remained unchanged towards 1900, as a critic noted in an 1899 issue of *L'Art Décoratif*, 'What do we see on every side? Wallpapers which wound the eye; against them, ornate furniture which wounds the eye; at intervals, a gaudily draped bay which wounds the eye; and every spare nook and cranny is hung with plates of spinach with decorative borders which wound the eye. Let the eye come to terms with all this as best it can.'

It was in part this Victorian preoccupation with a cluttered eclecticism – its *horror vacui* and outmoded taste – that in the 1890s opened the door to the concepts of modern interior design through which Art Nouveau advanced one of its own causes, that of neat and coherent settings for the home. Henry van de Velde explained the breakthrough in *Formule d'une Esthétique Moderne*, 'Reason is revolted by this perennial cowardice, this persistent refusal to seek out the right form, the form which is simple, truthful, and absolute.'

The Art Nouveau solution, exemplified for the public in the modern *ensembles* displayed by department stores and at the annual Salons, was to synchronize every element of a room, from its general colour scheme to the smallest detail of its smallest object, such as the key escutcheons and hinges on its furniture. Everything had to be *en suite*, in total contrast to the typical *recherché* interiors of the time. Today, nearly all those Art Nouveau interiors have gone, their wallpapers and upholstery long since faded or stripped, and the suites of furniture dispersed within families or at auction. Even surviving hand-tinted prints and glass chromolithographs fail fully to reveal the ambience of harmony and intimacy sought by their Art Nouveau designers. Yet enough has survived to show that in this aspect of

1 William Morris, *Bird*, wool hanging, 1879–80

design, at least, the new movement offered a radical improvement on the *status quo*.

It is to William Morris that Art Nouveau owed its single greatest debt. Far earlier, and far more stridently, than any other individual or group, it was Morris who challenged mid-Victorian aesthetic values and the manner in which they affected society as a whole. Like Ruskin before him, Morris did not always practise what he preached, but it was what he preached that mattered and which led, ultimately, to the climate of changing expectations that swept the United Kingdom and Europe in the 1880s and 1890s. In its most exuberant manifestations,

Art Nouveau certainly over-reached the revolution in household design for which Morris had striven, yet his teachings continued to serve and guide it.

The Industrial Revolution provided the focus of Morris's discontent. Through it, mankind had lost its soul and become engulfed in a morass of inexpensive mass-production that deadened its sensibilities, while cheapening life itself. Even a cursory glance at the international exhibition catalogues of the time – those in 1851, 1855, 1862, 1867, and 1878 – reveal the grounds for Morris's concern: page after page of shabbily made wares imitative of other ages and cultures.

Morris condemned any use whatsoever of the machine, and also the excessive division of labour that it entailed. Human beings needed an environment conducive to both physical and spiritual health. To Morris, therefore, the machine was innately evil, as it destroyed beauty and debased civilization. In search of a model lifestyle by which to remedy the situation, he chose the Middle Ages over Classical Antiquity and the Renaissance. Morris was no doubt manufacturing a legend in his depiction of the medieval craftsman as free and happy, but this romanticized vision inspired the group of disciples who quickly rallied to his reformist banner. The Gothic period, therefore, became the model for a new Age of Faith, Reason, Chivalry and, especially, the Craftsman. 'Paradise Regained' became the refrain of the craft movements spawned through Morris's exhortations, first in England and then in Europe and the United States.

A major contradiction in Morris's medievalizing doctrines – forgiven or ignored by artist-craftsmen in their eagerness to pursue his teachings – was that if one rejects the machine, one cannot produce cheaply. He was, nevertheless, successful in persuading the art community – painters, architects and artisans alike – to revert to an honourable tradition of household production, one which to him was a matter also of social conscience.

Morris's own designs displayed an enlightened traditionalism. Whereas certain Elizabethan and Jacobean sympathies are evident, particularly in his wall hangings and embroideries, his designs were essentially original. His choice of a botanical decorative vernacular, together with his glorification of handcraftsmanship, provided the dual foundation on which the European Art Nouveau movement was built. The next generation of Morris's countrymen, however – including Charles Voysey, Ernest Archibald Taylor, Ernest Newton, Charles R. Ashbee and Halsey Ricardo – resisted the ultra-stylizations introduced in his name by their Belgian and French counterparts, preferring the more understated, essentially sensible and solid, stylistic interpretations espoused by the English Arts and Crafts and Aesthetic Movements.

If Morris was the theoretician whose beliefs more than those of anyone else initiated the Art Nouveau movement, it was Arthur Heygate Mackmurdo (1851–1942), the English architect, graphic artist, craftsman and (later) economist, who provided its earliest practical implementation in the field of design. Mackmurdo's designs were in marked contrast to anything in Europe at the time. Two elements, in particular, established him as an unprecedented talent: his pursuit of linear simplicity and his asymmetrical compositions rendered in boldly contrasting colours, such as black and white. His choice of plant motifs, and the manner of their abstraction, likewise set him apart from his contemporaries.

His revolutionary chair-back of around 1883 precipitated the *fin-de-siècle* decorative movement. The fretwork splat, comprised of a row of slender tendrils tossed by the wind, is readily perceivable by today's observer as a pivotal Art Nouveau influence. The interplay

2

2 Arthur Heygate Mackmurdo, chair, *c.* 1883

between the apparent movement in the foreground and the stationary background creates a *trompe l'oeil* effect that provides the composition with endless rhythm and motion, like seaweed caught in opposing currents. This pre-occupation with movement became a hallmark of turn-of-the-century design.

Mackmurdo's first graphic expression of Art Nouveau is generally accepted as his title-page for *Wren's City Churches*, published by G. Allen in 1883. In this radical composition, arabesque ornament is integrated with the typography to create the same sense of movement found in the chair-back. This became a standard element in Mackmurdo's two-dimensional designs, in most of which the stylized images – some interpreted by contemporary critics as tongues of flame, or flame-like, rather than botanical – appear to float against a background of air or water, in which they sway from side to side in perpetual motion. This combination of rigorously flat surfaces, undulating plant forms, and contrasting colours anticipated the mature graphic syntax of Art Nouveau by fifteen years, and is today indistinguishable from much of it.

Mackmurdo designed illustrations and typography for *Hobby Horse*, a journal published first by the Century Guild in 1884, and again between 1886 and 1892. This aspect of his work, which was hailed at the 1886 Liverpool exhibition as the most advanced in Europe, had practically no impact on that of his compatriots. C.F.A. Voysey, M.H. Baillie-Scott, Ernest Gimson, C.R. Ashbee and George Walton, among others, were inspired far more by the restraint and rationality found in the stalk-like perpendicular struts of his architecture and furniture than the proto-Art Nouveau floral abstractions of his works on paper. For these, there were no English disciples, whereas on the Continent two Germans, Hermann Olbrist and Otto Eckmann, and two Belgians, Henry van de Velde and Georges Lemmen, heralded the eager reception awaiting Mackmurdo's innovations there.

Mackmurdo exposed his readers to the works of an even earlier
3   precursor of Art Nouveau, the poet and illustrator William Blake (1757–1827). Blake's wood engravings and temperas for *Songs of Innocence* (1789) and *Whirlwind of Lovers* (1824-27) were reproduced in *Hobby Horse*. His smoothly flowing and undulating linear style of ornamentation, and the manner in which he integrated it with the text and then both within the margins of the page, clearly established him as *the* proto-Art Nouveau artist. In *Songs of Innocence* especially, Blake revealed a vigorous organic style of typographic decoration in

Sweet masking May, in white or
red,
Her snowy cloud of blossom
spread.

3 William Blake, relief etching tinted
with watercolour for the titlepage of
Songs of Innocence, 1789

4 Walter Crane, illustration
for *Flora's Feast*, 1889

which the simplified and flattened forms also showed his familiarity
with Japanese printmaking. Blake's vitality and expressiveness are
clearly evident both in Mackmurdo's designs and in those of *Hobby
Horse*.

The English designer and book illustrator Walter Crane (1845–
1915) was another to provide inspiration to the Art Nouveau
movement in its seminal years. Though he was not a particularly
gifted artist, Crane showed progressive skills as a designer of objects
across a broad spectrum of the applied arts, including ceramics,
fabrics, wallpapers, embroidery, book illustrations and stained glass,
which he produced from the late 1860s. Some of his designs have Pre-
Raphaelite and Renaissance tendencies, but his work on wallpapers
and children's books was fresh, if not sometimes over-sentimental and
prettified. His initial production of wallpapers, consisting of compact
Morris-inspired patterns of stylized trees or flowers interlaced with
birds or animals, drew early admiration on the Continent. It was,

however, in his illustrations for children's books – 'toy books', as these volumes of fairy tales and nursery rhymes were termed – that his use of a fanciful and lively pictorial style dominated by floral motifs can be seen as a direct antecedent to the Art Nouveau vocabulary of decorative ornament.

Flora's Feast, published in 1889, proved astonishingly avant-garde in its illustrations of a young woman, Flora, and flowers in hybrid compositions that depict her calling them from their winter sleep. Flora, enveloped in daffodils, anemones and lilies, and with her hair swept by the wind, forms a series of graceful *femme-fleur* images which today's observer can be forgiven for presuming, erroneously, they had made their debut at the Paris Salons some fifteen years later. Crane's flat rendering and choice of harmonious colours in these illustrations also showed his affinity for *Japonisme*, a further bond linking his work to that of the Art Nouveau graphic artist. Two later works, *Illustrations for Shakespeare* (1893–94) and *The Shepheard's Calendar* (1895), firmly established Crane's reputation overseas.

Crane shared the belief of his friend William Morris in handcrafts-manship over industrialization, and he too embraced the Socialist philosophies which this embodied. His contributions to the cause were significant: in 1884 he founded The Art Worker's Guild, and four years later, in association with Lewis F. Day, The Arts and Crafts Exhibition Society. His goal of 'turning our artists into craftsmen and our craftsmen into artists' was reiterated by Henry van de Velde when he carried the English message across the Channel.

In 1911, well after the *de facto* disappearance of Art Nouveau in Europe, Crane repudiated the movement in his memoirs, *William Morris to Whistler*, referring to it as 'that strange decorative disease'. Like other of his compatriots who had been quick to place themselves in the vanguard of the new movement, and who had sought thereby to take credit for its early successes, Crane claimed later to be appalled by its vulgar commercial manifestations, and moved to dissociate himself from it as fully as possible.

Another source of incalculable impact in Art Nouveau's evolution was *Japonisme*, which became the rage in fashionable Western society following the treaty between the United States and Japan drawn up by Commodore Matthew C. Perry in February 1854. Traditionally, the distinction between Japanese and Chinese art had been blurred in Europe; most goods imported from the Far East were labelled broadly as 'Oriental', or in *le gout Chinois*. Decoration for the home, such as the *Vernis Martin* quasi-lacquered furniture revived by 19th-century

Parisian cabinetmakers, drew readily on the artistic iconography of both countries. The confusion between the two cultures was somewhat remedied, however, by Perry's treaty with the shogun, which led to the quick implementation of trade agreements between Japan and the principal Western powers.

Western artists drew on a host of compositional devices used by their Japanese counterparts, particularly the two-dimensional picture frame, flattened perspectives (often from a bird's-eye view), block colours and silhouetting. *Japonisme* even extended, in some instances, to the introduction by artists and designers – Toulouse-Lautrec, Whistler, Georges Auriol and Emile Gallé, among others – of Japanese-style cartouches and calligraphy as a means of signing their work.

Inspiration was available to the Western artist and decorator in a host of Japanese art works, including *Ukiyo-e* prints, woodcuts and lacquerware by such masters as Katsushika Hokusai (1760–1849), Ando Hiroshige (1797–1858) and Kitagawa Utamaro (1753–1806). In particular, Hokusai's *Mangwa* print album became a primary source for Japanese motifs and their interrelationship within a composition on the printed page. Japanese fans, ceramics, enamelwares, masks, screens, and kimonos likewise proved a ready source of inspiration as they flooded Europe from the mid-1850s. By the time of the 1862 London Exhibition, and again at the 1867 Exposition Universelle in Paris, this orientation – literally – was in full swing throughout Europe.

The Japanese artist drew his inspiration from nature, which Western painters were quick to assimilate into their work. Bamboos, carp, wisteria, cherry blossoms and waterlilies gained prominence in the West's decorative repertoire, as did the Japanese artist's predilection for a muted palette and emphasis on the poetic quality of nature. Many imitators emerged, in both the fine and the applied arts; in fact, a profound Oriental influence can be seen in virtually every discipline within the Art Nouveau movement. Only architecture (with the noted exception of Horta) and sculpture escaped its impact to a significant degree.

Among Japan's most enthusiastic proselytizers were Siegfried Bing and Arthur Lasenby Liberty, two merchants who were destined later to play giant roles in the dissemination and marketing of the Art Nouveau movement in the decorative arts.

Bing, a naturalized Frenchman from Hamburg, visited Japan in 1875, and then established an emporium for Japanese goods at 19 rue

5 Ando Hiroshige, *Plum trees in flower*, woodcut, 1857

6 Liberty & Company, roller-printed cotton, *c.* 1894

Chauchat, Paris (later expanded around the corner to 22 rue de Provence, where he opened his Maison Art Nouveau). From 1888 Bing also published a journal, *Le Japon Artistique*, which included articles on all aspects of Japanese life.

The career of Arthur Lasenby Liberty (1843–1917) was remarkably similar to that of Bing. Placed in charge of an Oriental warehouse filled with the purchases of a London firm, Farner & Rogers, Liberty developed a deep affection for Japanese art. In 1874, when the firm closed, he acquired its outstanding inventory, and the following year opened his own shop on Regency Street. His stock comprised a fine selection of Japanese silks, linens and printed cottons, which drew the attention, among others, of the Pre-Raphaelites and Whistler. In 1889, after a visit to the Far East and in order to capitalize on the prospect of the Exposition Universelle in Paris, Liberty opened a branch on that city's avenue de l'Opéra. The store remained in operation until 1931.

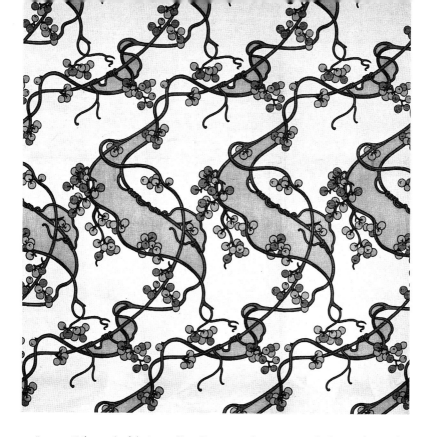

It was Liberty's fabrics – first Japanese imports and, from the early 6
1890s, in the emerging modernist idiom – more than its selection of
household products, that propelled his store to international fame. In
the 1890s particularly, Liberty became a status symbol for Europe's
fashion elite, helping greatly to spread the message and to establish the
legitimacy of the new movement's curvilinear grammar of ornament. Many of the initial designs were reminiscent of Mackmurdo's,
but by 1896 they had developed an individuality which inspired a host
of similar wallpaper and upholstery patterns among the firm's
competitors on the Continent.

A cocky and pretentious aesthete, the American expatriot James
Abbott McNeill Whistler (1834–1903) was the first major painter in
London to show a direct Japanese influence, both in his work and in
his lifestyle. His canvas *La Princesse du Pays de la Porcelaine* of 1863–64 7
reveals his early affinity for Japanese woodcuts and their interplay of
space and outline to generate a sophisticated simplicity. His famous

pseudo-Japanese butterfly monogram, resembling those used by Oriental printmakers, emphasized his unashamed enthusiasm for the refined beauty of Japanese art.

Too much of an individualist to be part of any circle, Whistler was nevertheless friendly with the Pre-Raphaelites, with whom he shared his enthusiasm for Japanese art. Beardsley, too, was greatly infuenced by him. In 1863, and again in 1867, Whistler decorated his house in the Japanese manner, selecting a harmonious blend of lemon yellows, pearly whites, flesh pinks and gold for his silk upholstery and wallpapers. The sparse white-lacquered furnishings were in the Anglo-Japanese taste, accentuated with gold-leaf, and set off against matching white dados. His Peacock Room of 1876–77, commissioned by the shipping magnate F. R. Leyland to house his porcelain collection in his London residence, brought Whistler international acclaim for its sumptuous exoticism. The room was remarkable both for its anticipation of the universal popularity that the peacock was to enjoy as a decorative motif at the turn of the century, and for its strong vertical emphasis – adopted later, among others, by Koloman Moser, Adolf Loos and other Viennese Secessionists.

Whistler's celebrity extended to the Continent, and particularly to Brussels, where he was invited by the members of the society called Les Vingt to participate in every exhibition held by them between 1884 and 1894. By this means he exerted a strong influence on the avant-garde Belgian School, which helped to fan the flames of *Japonisme* and to reinforce its impact on the movement away from conventionalism in art.

The career of Art Nouveau's *enfant terrible*, Aubrey Vincent Beardsley (1872–98), resembled that of the movement itself, springing up suddenly and brilliantly before moving through a variety of modifications, and then ceasing as abruptly as it had begun. In 1891, when he was nineteen years old, he paid Sir Edward Burne-Jones a visit to show him a portfolio of his drawings. Encouraged by the celebrated Pre-Raphaelite's response, he quit his job as an insurance clerk to try his hand as a graphic artist, a field in which he was entirely self-taught. His illustrations in Indian ink the following year for Sir Thomas Malory's *Morte d'Arthur*, some 350 in number, revealed both his indebtedness to Japanese printmaking in his use of flat decorative patterns, and the stark distinction between his mordant depiction of life in Camelot and the idealized vision of medieval chivalry espoused by Morris and his followers.

Within a year, Beardsley had matured into an accomplished

18

7 James Abbott McNeill Whistler,
La Princesse du Pays de la Porcelaine, 1863–64

draughtsman in complete control of line and concept. His illustrations
for Oscar Wilde's *Salome* showed his mastery of *Japoniste* techniques.
It was evident that he had an advanced understanding of how to
balance the flat, black areas of a composition with the negative white
spaces that separated them. A delicate, yet bold and dynamic,
network of lines writhe or sweep across the page, engulfing and
unifying neighbouring forms. So effective was Beardsley in the use of
this device that it is often difficult for the eye to differentiate between
what he drew and what he left out. Bookbindings and posters
extended the range of his creativity, but in these his designs were less
forceful, showing stylistic echoes of Blake and Mackmurdo.

Beardsley's notoriety did not, however, arise from his skills as a
graphic artist, but rather from the macabre character of his subject-
matter. His renderings evoked life's more sinister aspects, those which
Victorian society deemed taboo: perversion, eroticism, corruption
and depravity. Beardsley's pornographic illustrations for a private
edition of Aristophanes's bawdy play, *Lysistrata*, commissioned by
the entrepreneur Leonard Smithers, revealed the extent to which he
was prepared to flout the hypocritical standards of his times.

Within three years of setting out on his new career, Beardsley had
hit full stride. In 1884, he was appointed editor of *The Yellow Book*, a
position from which he was dismissed the following year in the
aftermath of Oscar Wilde's highly publicized trial and conviction.
Editorship of a newly founded journal, *The Savoy*, followed; he
contributed satirical drawings that endeared him to a sophisticated
readership of Aesthetes, Symbolists, Decadents, and other self-
ordained members of the *fin-de siècle* intellectual avant-garde.

Beardsley's meteoric career ended with his death in 1898, at the age
of 25. His impact on his peers had been profound and widespread;
they included Klimt in Vienna, Bradley in Chicago, Horta and van de
Velde in Brussels, Toorop in Amsterdam, Vallotton in Paris, Bakst in
St Petersburg, and 'The Four' in Glasgow – to name only the most
famous, in whose work his influence is readily evident. Many others,
particularly in the poster field, found inspiration in his provocative
genius.

Mackmurdo's revolutionary stylizations first crossed the Channel
to Brussels, where they drew the admiration of that city's community
of avant-garde artists, who exhibited jointly from 1884 through Les
Vingt. The inaugural showing was auspicious in its solicitation of the
epoch's sculpture sensation, Auguste Rodin. Formed under the
leadership of a local lawyer, Octave Maus, who sought out

8 Aubrey Vincent Beardsley, illustration for Oscar Wilde's *Salome*, 1894

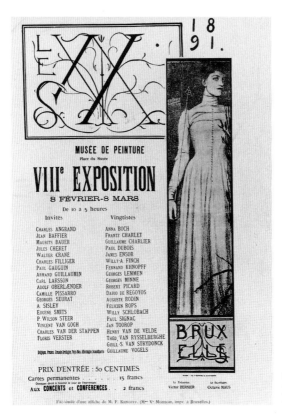

9 Fernand Khnopff,
poster for the exhibition
of Les Vingt, 1891

progressive works of art throughout Europe as a means to counteract historicism in Belgium, Les Vingt provided a forum for those whose works were barred by the juries who monitored entries to the traditional Salons. (Coincidentally, the Salon of La Société des Artistes Indépendants was established in Paris for the same reason in the same year.) Toorop, Ensor, Khnopff, Henry van de Velde, and Theo van Rysselberghe were among the society's charter members, which in 1892 permitted a range of decorative arts, probably for the first time, to be shown on equal terms with paintings and sculpture. A survey of the participants, who included Morris, Whistler and Beardsley, reveals the powerful influence exerted on the Belgians by the English decorative arts movement. Georges Lemmen's cover for the society's 1891 catalogue, a moonlit seascape rendered in swirling lines of water and light that swelled and shrank as they meandered across the composition, borrowed shamelessly from Mackmurdo.

In his cover design for the 1890 exhibition catalogue, Khnopff gave evidence of the influence of Japanese art and calligraphy on the group.

In 1894, Les Vingt was dissolved and re-established as La Libre Esthétique, which continued to promote and exhibit what it determined as progressive art, not only canvases by such artists as Seurat, Signac, Toulouse-Lautrec, Gauguin and Redon, but also applied works and furniture by Alexandre Charpentier, Ashbee, Rupert Carabin, Henri Cros and Tiffany, and the work of some of the host nation's most gifted artist-designers: Philippe Wolfers, Victor Rousseau, Constantin Meunier and Gustave Serrurier-Bovy. A decade later, Art Nouveau's impetus among its members was spent; the 1904 exhibition introduced a series of displays consecrated to other themes in art.

The 'New Art' movement assumed many national and regional names as it took root and burgeoned in Europe, creating for the period's critics and later historians the need to settle on a phrase that would encompass as fully as possible its modernist aims and varied facets. In France, it was described initially as *Le Modern Style* rather than the Gallic *Art Nouveau* – coined in most part by foreign critics to describe the type of furnishings offered by Siegfried Bing in his Maison Art Nouveau gallery in Paris – by which the movement gradually became known everywhere. The decorative arts periodicals that proliferated throughout Europe during the 1890s, such as *Pan*, *Art et Décoration*, *L'Art Décoratif*, *The Studio*, *Jugend*, *Deutsche Kunst und Dekoration*, and *Mir Isskustva*, helped to familiarize readers with the Art Nouveau movement, and to standardize the terms and vernacular associated with it.

Predictably, the movement's local characteristics often determined its nomenclature; for example, it was referred to variously in Germany as *Jugendstil* ('Youth Style', after the Munich magazine that was instrumental in its promotion, *Jugend*), *Lilienstil* ('Lily Style'), *Wellenstil* ('Wave Style'), and, with distinctly pejorative overtones, *Bandwurmstil* ('Tapeworm Style'); in Italy as *Stile Liberty* (after the London store), *Stile Floreal* ('Floral Style'), *Stile Nouille* ('Noodle Style'), and *Stile Vermicelli* ('Macaroni Style'); in Belgium, *Paling Stijl* ('Eel Style'); and in Austria, *Secession*. The Spanish term for the movement was perhaps most apposite: *Modernista*. Elsewhere, particularly in France, it was referred to variously as *Style Métro* (after Guimard's Underground entrances), Glasgow Style (after Charles Mackintosh and his group), and Yachting Style, used by Edmond de

Goncourt in his newspaper column to ridicule Bing's *ensembles* at the 1900 Exposition, which to him resembled ship interiors.

Well removed historically and geographically from the mainstream of French art, Nancy is the industrial hub and railhead of Alsace-Lorraine, two provinces that had been annexed by Germany in 1871. The city's pre-eminence in the French decorative arts at the *fin de siècle* was therefore dependent less on tradition than on the artistic achievements of its citizens, particularly Emile Gallé, who first came to prominence in the early 1880s. Gallé aspired to an alliance of the region's industrial arts, and following his success at the 1889 Exposition Universelle, during which his stylistic innovations in glass and furniture were greeted with international acclaim, he became the catalyst for his fellow artisans. This loosely knit group presented a united front at the 1900 Exposition Universelle, where its triumphs were legion, under the banner of the Ecole de Nancy. Here Gallé was joined by a score of his Nancéien colleagues, some of whom likewise became household names in their respective fields. Included were Louis Majorelle, Eugène Vallin, Jacques Gruber and Camille Gauthier in furniture design and manufacture, the Daum *frères* in glass, René Wiener in leather, the Mougin *frères* in ceramics, and, a generation older than his *confrères* and acting therefore in the capacity of artistic counsel and collaborator to all, the mixed-media artist Victor Prouvé.

The Ecole de Nancy was formally, and somewhat belatedly, incorporated the following year. Gallé was elected president, with Prouvé, Majorelle and Daum as vice-presidents. Its charter, published in the *Bulletin des Sociétés Artistiques de l'Est*, listed its goals: to create a professional school of instruction for the industrial arts; to found a museum, library and permanent collection; to organize conferences; to publish a bulletin; and to arrange expositions and competitions for its members. Two further group shows, in 1903 in Paris and the following year in Nancy, provided additional high points in the School's brief existence. Gallé's death at the end of 1904 signalled the start of its decline, which continued until the 1909 Exposition de l'Est de France; after that the School passed into history. Its choice of a floral anthology, comprised mostly of local species recreated in profusion on all its works, quickly outstayed its initial welcome.

The Ecole de Nancy's interpretation of Art Nouveau differed sharply from that of the movement's other European adherents. In Nancy, nature was depicted with fierce realism; elsewhere, it was subject to a stylization that ran the gamut from subtle (Brussels and Paris) to complex (Glasgow and Vienna).

10 Emile Gallé, marquetry table top, 1890s

In Paris, the momentum of Art Nouveau was maintained from the early 1890s largely by Siegfried Bing. Bing's infatuation with the Far East had been overtaken from around the time of the 1889 Exposition Universelle by his exposure to the incipient movement, both in Europe and in the United States, where, on a visit to the 1893 Columbian Exposition in Chicago, he made the acquaintance of Louis Comfort Tiffany. The meeting led to a business partnership that proved mutually beneficial – for Bing, the opportunity to represent America's foremost decorative artist in Paris, and for Tiffany an agent through whose gallery his creations in glass would reach the overseas audience that he lacked.

Bing opened his Maison Art Nouveau in December 1895, with an exhibition of ten windows designed by members of the Nabis – including Toulouse-Lautrec, Pierre Bonnard, Paul Ranson, Félix Vallotton, Edouard Vuillard and Henri Ibels – which were executed by Tiffany in New York with his magical Favrile glass. The gallery quickly established itself as *the* Parisian mouthpiece for the new movement, where the recent works of van de Velde, Beardsley, Lalique, Colonna, Gaillard and de Feure could also be seen.

The 1900 Exposition Universelle provided Bing with the vehicle of his greatest triumph. His pavilion comprised a series of *ensembles* 11

11 Poster for Bing's Maison Art Nouveau, c. 1900

12 Edouard Colonna's room for Siegfried Bing's Art Nouveau pavilion at the 1900 Exposition Universelle.

12   designed by his three top designers: Colonna, de Feure and Gaillard. Bing understood that it was a room's general ambience, rather than its individual components, that would create a lasting impression. To this end, each interior presented a harmonious whole in which everything – the furniture, fabrics, tableware, wallpaper, ceramics and miscellaneous *objets d'art* – was *en suite*, both in style and in colour. The Parisian public, conditioned to the congested historicism of the city's average apartment, were awed by what they saw as refined and disciplined. Others, however, were less impressed. Dr Max Osborn, a German critic, summarized his countrymen's dislike of French Art Nouveau in the scarcely concealed sarcasm of his review of Bing's pavilion for *Deutsche Kunst und Dekoration*, 'For us Germans [the *Art Nouveau*] is a bit too feminine, too whimsical, too *cocotte*. For the French, perhaps, exactly what they desire.'

The Maison Art Nouveau closed in 1904. When Bing died the following year, the movement to which he had given its name was in rapid retreat.

Another German, the art critic Julius Meier–Graefe, adopted a role of entrepreneur and patron parallel to Bing's in the French capital. A devotee of modern art, he sought to apply it in a coherent manner to

every aspect of interior design. In 1898 he opened a gallery, La Maison Moderne, in the rue des Petits-Champs through which to showcase furnishings designed and manufactured in his workshops. In its accumulative talent, his team of designers matched that of the Maison Art Nouveau. Included were van de Velde, Abel Landry, Paul Follot, Maurice Dufrène and Emmanuel Orazi.

The economic fortunes of La Maison Moderne were linked inextricably with the popularity of the Art Nouveau movement at the Paris Salons. The gallery flourished around the time of the 1900 Exposition Universelle, only to plummet three years later. (It closed around the same time that Bing's did). For some of its designers, however – particularly Follot and Dufrène – the gallery provided an invaluable springboard for their own careers.

In Germany, there was one early and seemingly isolated design in the *Jugendstil* by Hermann Obrist (1863–1927), who in 1894 transferred his embroidery workshop from Florence to Munich. One of his wall hangings from this period, entitled 'Cyclamen', was decorated with a single silk flower laid out in a series of sharply curving lines and loops, whose frantic movement reminded a critic on Berlin's *Pan* magazine of 'the sudden violent curves generated by the

13

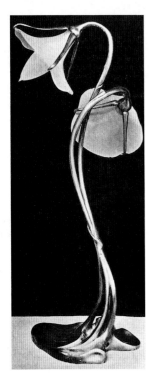

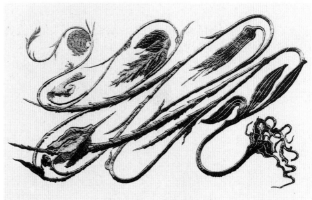

14 Hermann Obrist, *The Whiplash*, wall hanging, 1892–94

13 Maurice Dufrène, bronze lamp
shown in the 1901 Salon of the
Société des Artistes Décorateurs

14 crack of a whip'. This opinion was so widely published at the time that the wall hanging became known as 'The Whiplash'.

An artist's colony in Darmstadt was another German project that helped to consolidate and legitimize the new movement. In 1899, the young Grand Duke Ernst Ludwig of Hesse invited seven German and Austrian artists – Peter Behrens, Rudolf Bosselt, Paul Burck, Hans Christiansen, Ludwig Habich, Patriz Huber and Joseph M. Olbrich – 15 to form a permanent community for artists, called Mathildenhöhe, in Darmstadt, for which Behrens designed all but one of the buildings. (Olbrich designed his own residence.) The Duke's inspiration came from the English Arts and Crafts Movement, with whose manifesto he had no doubt become familiar during his association with Baillie-Scott, who designed furniture for him in 1898. The group's first presentation was at the 1900 Exposition Universelle, which was followed in October the next year with the official inaugural exhibition, entitled 'A Document of German Art', at Mathildenhöhe, and participation in both the 1902 Turin Exposition and the 1904 World's Fair in St. Louis.

15 Peter Behrens, house on the Mathildenhöhe estate, Darmstadt, 1901

The attention afforded the English Arts and Crafts Movement in Darmstadt was shared elsewhere in Germany. Of the numerous craft societies that sprang up in the country during the 1880s and 1890s, it was the one in Munich that had the greatest impact on future design. The Deutsche Werkstätte, founded there in 1897 by Karl Schmidt, was in the vanguard of the international movement that evolved at the turn of the century away from the concept of handcraftsmanship and towards that of serial production. For the Germans, the issue was confronted and clearly defined well before it was elsewhere in Europe or in England: should the Morris tradition of the individual craftsman continue to be upheld and consolidated, or should it yield to an industrialized form of manufacture based on standardized components (*Typenmöbel*)? The debate was, of course, fundamental to that facing the Art Nouveau designer at the time: how to reconcile (if at all) individual versus industrial design.

The formation in Munich in 1907 of the Deutsche Werkbund sealed the fate of the individual German craftsman, if not immediately then by the outbreak of World War I. The society's founder, Hermann Muthesius (1861–1927), invited a group of industrialists to assist in formulating for it standards of mass production appropriate to the new machine age; hindsight shows that these were a watershed in the history of modern design. The Werkbund's full impact extends beyond the scope of this book, except to note that its spartan, functional ideology led directly to that of Gropius and the Bauhaus which, although founded barely two decades after the high point of *Jugendstil*, seems much further removed in both time and concept.

In Vienna, the focus was different from that in Munich. There the issue was how to unite art and industry in the common battle against mass-produced mediocrity, rather than against the craftsman. It was felt that good and honest handcraft, rather than machine-age production, was essential to the moral and economic well-being of the nation. If handcraftsmanship could ally itself with modern means of manufacture – specifically, the machine – then quality could be maintained and costs controlled to achieve an acceptable compromise. If not the best of both worlds, in effect, then at least a workable union.

Otto Wagner (1841–1918), head of the School of Architecture at the Vienna Academy of Fine Art, became the *éminence grise* of the Secession movement, formed in 1897 – the most influential of several progressive schools that had sprung up in the city towards 1900 to foment and implement change. Under Wagner's influence were Josef

Hoffmann and Koloman Moser, both pioneers of the Secession movement and faculty members of the city's Kunstgewerbeschule, who in 1903 established the Wiener Werkstätte, a set of cooperative workshops through which to realize a marriage of Austrian art and industry at the highest level. Galvanized by the work of Charles Rennie Mackintosh, which was displayed at the Secession's eighth exhibition in 1900, and again the following year in a German competition, 'Haus eines Kunstfreundes', Hoffmann and Moser set out to create a Viennese decorative idiom based on that of the Glaswegian. Rejected fully were the flowers and lissome nymphs favoured by the French Art Nouveau and German *Jugendstil* movements; in their place, a crisp and slender angularity dominated by geometric patterns, including the chequerboard matrix which became Hoffmann's stylistic signature (he was known among his colleagues as *Quadratl*-Hoffmann). An entrepreneur, Fritz Warndorfer, was persuaded to finance the venture.

In flagrant contempt of Morris's pronouncements on the needs of the common man, the Wiener Werkstätte aimed from the outset to serve a wealthy, sophisticated and cosmopolitan clientele. Until World War I their production included a glittering array of furniture,

16 Josef Hoffmann, desk, *c.* 1901

metalware, ceramics, textiles and jewelry, in patterns that anticipated the stylistic idiosyncrasies of the late 1920s and 1930s. Even today, many of these appear startlingly modern.

The outbreak of hostilities in 1914 brought an end to these brilliant achievements. The deaths in 1918 of four of Vienna's modernist giants – Gustav Klimt, Otto Wagner, Egon Schiele and Koloman Moser – served further to signify the end of a glorious era. And although the Wiener Werkstätte remained in operation until 1931, the output grew increasingly commercial and frivolous.

A felicitous blend of architectural talent and vision, on the one hand, and the public's dissatisfaction with the status quo, on the other, came together towards 1900 in Glasgow to provide a climate sympathetic to radical change. The city's new art movement was dominated by Charles Rennie Mackintosh, a young architect in the firm of John Honeyman & Keepie. Mackintosh introduced a highly distinctive grammar of decorative ornament into his designs for buildings and every facet of their interiors; this was based on rigorous perpendicularity adorned with attenuated roses, apple pips, trees and tulips. Later, images of ethereal maidens were introduced into his wallpapers and stencilled upholstery.

Assisting Mackintosh were Herbert MacNair, an associate at John Honeyman & Keepie, and two sisters, Margaret and Frances MacDonald, who married the two men (Margaret and Mackintosh in 1900; Frances and McNair the previous year). The group, which became known internationally as 'The Four', developed the Glasgow style, an important element of the new movement. Vienna, in particular, borrowed heavily on their novel brand of ornamentation.

Mackintosh's impact on 20th-century design was phenomenal, and out of all proportion to his brief career, which totally eclipsed those of the foremost architects to the south of Scotland. An anonymous contributor to *Our Homes and How to Beautify Them* expressed the typical English attitude in his review of a Mackintosh dining-room, 'The aesthetic movement in its maddest moments was never half so mad as this . . . the Scotto-Continental "New Art" threatens in its delirious fantasies to make the movement for novelty a target for the shafts of scoffers and a motive for the laughter of the saner seven-eights of mankind.'

The Glasgow School was effectively extinct by 1908, leaving the movement's protagonists quite unprepared for the loss of commissions and celebrity that followed. Mackintosh suffered its effect more than the others; he ended in genteel poverty in the South of France,

17

DAS SPEISE-ZIMMER.

17 Charles Rennie Mackintosh, dining room designed for the *Haus eines Kunstfreundes* competition, 1900–01

where from 1923 he eked out a living as a watercolourist. His architectural *oeuvre* was virtually forgotten for another forty years.

Isolated rumblings against Art Nouveau-inspired works of art – in particular, their persistent disregard for the fundamental principle of good design (that an object's ornamentation must always remain subservient to its function) – began in the late 1890s, and became a passionate outcry by 1905. Soon, a roving army of critics had formed to police the annual exhibitions in Paris, Brussels, Nancy and Munich, with the mission of curbing the movement's ill-considered exuberance. Logic, it was argued, was being sacrificed on the altar of Beauty.

One early warning was expressed at the moment of the movement's high point – the 1900 Exposition Universelle – by Charles Genuys, a critic for *La Revue des Arts Décoratifs*, who wrote, 'it is claimed that the *Art* called *Nouveau* consists of new forms substituted for other outmoded forms, yet it is forgotten that [the *Art Nouveau*], like its predecessors, must remain logical, well constructed, and observe the limitations imposed by the materials employed.' The comment seems now to have been directed especially at the furniture displays at the Exposition which, more than any other, drew the critics' disdain. The contents of one pavilion at the Exposition were described as both 'bizarre' and 'a bazaar'.

In 1904, the tone of an article by R. D. Benn in *Style in Furniture* typified that of the many critics who by then were openly challenging the various claims of legitimacy made for Art Nouveau by its protagonists. 'With regard to this "new art", it has been said, and with some measure of reason, that, on the one hand, most of it which is really new is not art, and, on the other, that which is art is not new; and I do not think that the situation could be summed up more correctly or concisely.'

Many years later, in 1951, in one of the first retrospective studies of the Art Nouveau movement, Henry F. Lenning wrote, 'After 1905–06, the *Art Nouveau* in France, and therefore in Belgium, loses its significance. It wanders off into other styles, becomes absorbed by the modern Baroque, and, in short, ceases to be a dynamic movement. Exhibitions were no longer devoted to it as a style, and show only certain design elements which lingered on as the movement faded rapidly from the creative horizon.' It is interesting to note that the Baroque style managed to survive for half a century, whereas the life span of Art Nouveau was only about fifteen years (1890–1905).

Contributing to the movement's rapid downfall was the fact that it had been promoted in large part by brilliant individualists – Horta, Gaudí, Mucha, Lalique and Gallé, to name just a few of its most gifted exponents – scattered throughout Europe. Its momentum had been fueled more by independent achievements, geographically dispersed and often isolated, than by a formal system of tuition, such as that provided by the Ecole des Beaux-Arts, which would have ensured a degree of stylistic continuity and standardization. The movement's very essence – its spontaneity and unbridled eccentricity – could neither be taught to the rank and file, nor copied by them with impunity. This accounts, in part, for the large volume of inferior decorative works – often *bibelots* and other household appurtenances – that flooded the market between 1900 and 1905, often by way of the annual Paris Salons. Four of these – the Salon d'Automne and those of the Société des Artistes Français, the Société Nationale des Beaux-Arts, and the Société des Artistes Décorateurs – served as the vehicle by which the work of many of those designers drawn to Art Nouveau because of its high visibility and chic appeal could reach the public. This was often promoted, too, by way of ceramic manufactories and bronze foundries, which purchased the right at the Salons to reproduce their work in large editions.

The surfeit of objects at the Salons exposed the inadequacies of the movement's average designer to an increasingly critical audience, which, although previously forgiving of its youthful transgressions, now perceived them as repetitious and hackneyed, and totally unchecked. Even Art Nouveau's most identifiable and cherished motifs began to jar on the eye: the ubiquitous dancing line seemed to reach out and strangle the viewer's sensibilities, while the Belle Epoque maiden suddenly appeared inherently evil, her long flowing tresses tormented rather than merely entwined or unkempt. The movement's more blatant *clichés*, of course, were even more abruptly dismissed.

By 1910, almost the only living traces of Art Nouveau in Paris could be found in Jules Aimé Lavirotte's newly constructed Ceramic Hotel and the faded floral compositions that lingered at the Salons. The movement was effectively over, its death as much self-induced as brought about by extraneous factors. The Salons were largely filled now with nondescript designs, sterile evocations of past styles, such as 'Louis Quinze', which made a brief return to respectability. Many later historians, in anticipation of the highly distinctive 'Art Deco' that emerged in the 1920s, labelled the 1908–14 years in the French capital as interim or 'transitional'.

Beyond Paris, where its initial success had been less pronounced, the movement's downfall was less precipitous. The denunciations in the press and by the public were matched by a gradual reduction in the percentage of Art Nouveau-type furnishings and works of art offered by manufacturers.

World War I formally brought the curtain down on the *fin-de-siècle* epoch. For later critics, it has also provided a neat division between 19th- and 20th-century decorative design. Art Nouveau is now perceived as a Victorian movement which, although it straddled the two centuries, was out of step with modern design concepts and developments, and therefore part of the earlier one.

The future of 20th-century design lay more with the disciples of the German Werkbund, Hoffmann, Behrens and Loos, than with those of Gaudí, Guimard and Gallé, as was quickly evident. Van de Velde's doctrine of individual artistic expression lost out to the standardization of Muthesius. The aftermath of the war ushered in a host of new schools, including those of the Bauhaus, de Stijl, the Union des Artistes Modernes (U.A.M.) and the International Style, each with its own interpretation of, and goals for, machine-age design.

A full century after its inception, today's critics can be far less hostile to Art Nouveau than their predecessors were. The earlier sentiments of betrayal and derision, which survived into the 1950s, have been replaced by those of curiosity and, increasingly, tolerance and appreciation. Art Nouveau's wilder follies can now be viewed, and excused, in a broader historical context. The movement played the role of an 'anti' or 'spoiler' movement, which in theory if not in practice helped to discard the outmoded conventions of 19th-century society and to clear the stage for the developments that followed with such rapidity after 1918. Seen in this light, Art Nouveau remains a cul-de-sac leading off from the historical mainstream of art and architecture, but a vital one nonetheless.

Perhaps the final test of an art movement's achievements lies in its durability in the marketplace. Here, Art Nouveau's success has been assured by the huge interest in the last decade by museums and collectors (the latter both private and corporate) in acquiring major works by Art Nouveau artist-designers. Auction rooms are thronged by those in pursuit of the era's masterworks, which lead to spiralling prices and an enhanced status for the movement as a whole. Recent publications and exhibitions on the movement and its individual exponents have added further respectability, as have trends in architecture in the 1980s that show a renewed appreciation for both relief and surface ornament.

CHAPTER TWO

Architecture

Often summarily dismissed in histories of world architecture, Art Nouveau architecture remains controversial, despite the fact that it has begun to gain a measure of respectability as the result of a spate of recent museum exhibitions. Its roots have been traced in part to the writings of Viollet-le-Duc, the French architectural theoretician, whose *Entretiens* was published in two volumes in 1863 and 1872. Viollet-le-Duc espoused a frank use of modern materials and the development of new forms of artistic expression as the way to overcome the limitations of past building styles. His importance to architects later in the century arose from his prophetic suggestion that one could erect an armature – a lightweight metal skeleton – and cover it with masonry. Employed in arched or cantilevered form, this armature would eliminate the need for traditional forms of structural reinforcement, such as vaulted ceilings and flying buttresses. Thirty years later, Louis Sullivan, Victor Horta, Francis Jourdain and Auguste Perret bore witness to Viollet-le-Duc's visionary genius.

The Belgian architect Victor Horta was one of Viollet-le-Duc's most brilliant disciples, and certainly the first to apply his formulae successfully in the Art Nouveau idiom. Horta used steel – the most recent engineering innovation of the late 19th century – as the armature of his structures. Disregarding his mentor's advice, however, he chose to expose rather than to conceal it, and he did so proudly and defiantly. As Maurice Rheims noted in *The Flowering of Art Nouveau*, 'his houses showed their muscles and viscera, as if an anatomist had presented a sketch not dead but alive; he left exposed everything which Haussmann's architects had been at pains to conceal.' The outstanding example of this was Horta's Maison du Peuple, commissioned by the Belgian Socialist Party as their headquarters. Completed in 1899 (and destroyed in 1965/66), the building revealed in its interior the entire infrastructure of stanchions, girders and stone imposts. These, together with the building's glass curtain walls and railings, were united aesthetically in Horta's highly distinctive modernist style.

Well before this, in 1892–93, Horta had dumbfounded the international architectural community with his design for an *hôtel particulier* (private residence) for Emile Tassel, a prosperous Brussels engineer and industrialist. The design seems to have caught everybody by surprise. One of Horta's former teachers, Alphonse Balat, was reported to have burst into tears on viewing it.

With the Tassel house, Horta brought the Art Nouveau concept in architecture to instant full maturity, and transferred it from the restricted realm of the decorative arts to a much larger scale. Surviving photographs show that the house was a *tour de force*, both in its novel architectural and in its ornamental devices. By placing the vestibules on stepped levels, Horta eliminated the endless corridors then in common use, thus ensuring that the individual rooms became independent entities. Spatial continuity and fluidity were provided between floors by a coiled line, which unified the building's interior and furnishings. Charged with power and grace, and as light as air, this line became Horta's famous *imprimatur*, the common denominator in all his subsequent Art Nouveau buildings – particularly the residences he designed in Brussels for Armand Solvay (1894–98), Edmond van Eetvelde (1897), O. Aubecq (1903) and himself (1898–1901; now the Horta Museum). Of these, the Solvay house, on the avenue Louise, survives as the architect's most integrated and innovative architectural entity. In addition to Viollet-le-Duc, there are clear Rococo and *Japoniste* influences, both, however, subtly abstracted and personalized.

Horta's clients were drawn from the cultural elite and bourgeois intelligentsia of the Belgian capital. This avant-garde was composed mainly of engineers and former colonials, who in the 1890s sought to modernize all aspects of society, including its art. Other architects responded to the challenge in their embrace of the Art Nouveau idiom, though none with such coherence and flair. Among them were Paul Hamesse, who showed a restrained Horta influence in his façade for the Ets A. Ameke department store building (*c.* 1903); Emile van Averbeke, who adopted the whiplash Horta line for the Maison du Peuple Libérale in Anvers (1898); and Paul Hankar. Others, again, opted for a more hesitant modernism, preferring to mix it with traditional or Beaux-Arts influences. Notable in this category were Alban Chambon, Paul Cauchie, Antoine Pompe and Paul Saintenoy.

Mention must also be made here of Henry van de Velde, who was self-taught as an architect. Most of his architectural commissions in Belgium were for private residences, including his own home,

18 Victor Horta, Hôtel Tassel, Brussels, 1892–93

Bloemenwerf, in Uccle (1895). Often heavy and overworked, with strong echoes of Voysey, his architectural essays were more successful in Germany, where the majority of his Art Nouveau-inspired commissions were executed, including interiors for the Folkwang Museum (1899–1900) and the Dresden exhibition of 1906. Two delightful Berlin interiors, for the Havana Company Cigar Shop (1899–1900) and the Haby Barber's Shop (1900–01) helped to redeem van de Velde's often dubious reputation as an architect.

Horta's Tassel house made its greatest impact in Paris, where Hector Guimard was quick to adapt its serpentine configurations into his own highly distinctive grammar of ornament. The result was an important body of architectural work rendered in a luxurious and plastic organic style, of which the entrances to the Paris Métro stations are today the most readily identifiable. Erected in 1900, these – particularly the enclosed ones, as at the Porte Dauphine – remind the viewer of Art Nouveau's frenzied impact on the French capital at the turn of the century.

Guimard applied the same abstracted plant gyrations to every element and contour of his buildings, including their furnishings. The most noteworthy of these were the Castel Béranger (1894–98), the Humbert de Romans concert hall (1898), the Hôtel Roy (1898) and, in Lille, the Maison Coilliot (1897–1900). Imbued with a sense of his own celebrity, Guimard irritated the art world by describing himself in interviews and on his business card as an '*Architect d'art*'.

Charles Plumet, in partnership with the interior designer Tony Selmersheim, likewise chose an abstract botanical curvilinear style as the way to give his buildings a modern accent. Clearly less confident than Guimard, however, Plumet concealed his appetite for the modern style by blending it with 18th-century effects. Whether intentional or not, his concern was well-considered; when Art Nouveau fell quickly from grace around 1905, his body of architectural work was spared the critics' harshest comments. Sadly, most of his Paris commissions, including the distinguished Hôtel du Havre, the Kohler chocolate shop, Maison Cadolle and the restaurant Edouard, have disappeared. Showing a similar conservatism, Jules Lavirotte designed some understated modernist buildings in Paris around 1900, including residences at 3 square Rapp (1899) and 34 avenue Wagram (1904).

Xavier Schoellkopf, a graduate of the Ecole des Beaux-Arts in Paris, pursued a more rigorous Art Nouveau imagery than any architect other than Guimard. His house for the singer Yvette

19 Henry van de Velde,
Havana Company Cigar
Shop, Berlin, 1899–1900

20 Hector Guimard,
interior of his own
residence, 122 avenue
Mozart, Paris, c. 1910

41

Guilbert, for instance, incorporated a well-controlled pastiche of modern motifs. Energetic, but sometimes excitable, Schoellkopf was often judged by the critics to have allowed his youthful enthusiasm to run off into superfluities.

Many of the most rampantly Art Nouveau structures in Paris were designed by relatively obscure architects working on low budgets. Included in this category were a host of brasseries, patisseries, restaurants and cafés. In many instances, the commission was restricted to the shop front; in others, such as Maxim's (Louis Marnez, architect, in association with the painter Leon Sonnier) and Georges Fouquet's jewelry store (Alphonse Mucha), the façade's high-style ornamentation was extended into the interior. Somewhat in the same category of commercial projects that were expected to be short-lived was Henri Sauvage's pavilion for Loïe Fuller at the 1900 Exposition Universelle. Placing a full-relief figure of the American dancer over the central entrance, Sauvage embellished the pavilion's front façade with radiating bands of her billowing robes carved in high relief.

In Nancy, predictably, the Art Nouveau idiom was adopted by some of the city's architects to complement the interiors and decorative objects by which the Ecole de Nancy had brought it momentary fame. The most interesting designs were those of Emile André, who merged a quaint neo-Gothic provincialism with

21 Xavier Schoellkopf, fireplace for Yvette Guilbert's house, c. 1905

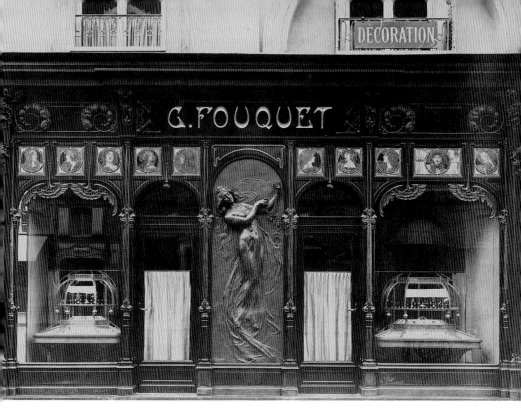

22 Alphonse Mucha, façade for Georges Fouquet's jewelry store, c. 1900

modernist impulses in a series of local houses. Some of these, such as the Maison Huot at 92–93a quai Claude-le-Lorrain and 30 avenue Sergent-Blandan (both 1903), and his villa 'Les Glycines' (1902), survive as monuments to the city's brief flirtation with international acclaim. Also noteworthy were residences designed by Lucien Weissenburger and the firm of Biet & Vallin. Sauvage's house for Louis Majorelle (1902), named the Villa Jika, remains an architectural curiosity due to its blend of medieval and Art Nouveau contours and imagery.

In Vienna, it was Otto Wagner and his gifted students, Hoffmann and Olbrich, who led the attempt to modernize architecture. 24 Wagner's association with the Secessionist movement is ambiguous, however; although some of his designs do qualify as radical, they were applied to structures of traditional form. Included in this category was his design for the Majolikahaus (1898), in which the façade was

43

23 Emile André, house in quai Claude-le-Lorrain, Nancy, 1903

garnished with radiating bands of brightly coloured red flowers on trailing stems. Similarly arresting was his design for the Karlsplatz railway station (1899–1900), which was enhanced by a frieze of formalized yellow sunflowers.

Olbrich's Secessionist style divides roughly into early and late stages. His initial architectural designs – from 1898 to 1904 – are charming and colourful, sometimes almost playful. His private residences – for example, the Villas Friedmann (1898), Bahr (1899–1900), Stifft (1899), and the Berl house (1899) – incorporate curvilinear contours and a liberal use of colourful floral surface ornamentation evocative both of Paris and of German *Jugendstil*. Included in his early period, but more formal because of its intended function, was his design in 1898 for the Secessionist group's own exhibition building, characterized by its large spherical cupola of openwork leaves. Olbrich's more mature works reveal an increasing conservatism, with the noted exception of his celebrated *Hochzeitsturm* (Wedding Tower) in Darmstadt (1905–08).

44

Inspired by Mackintosh, Hoffmann determined after 1900 to replace the new art movement's curves and fancies with slender verticals and smooth unbroken surfaces. His earlier buildings in Vienna, however, showed the same colourful intimacy and curvilinearity used at the time by Olbrich; for example, his façades for the Apollo candle shop and the Haus auf der Bergerhöhe (both 1899), and his interior for the Vienna School of Handicraft's pavilion at the 1900 Exposition Universelle in Paris. Between 1904 and 1910, however, Hoffmann pursued an increasingly severe architectural style, as in his 1904 designs for the Purkersdorf Sanatorium, west of Vienna, and the Villa Beer-Hofmann (1906), on which his earlier ornamental elements were sharply curtailed, if not entirely eliminated.

Hoffmann's most spectacular commission, executed in conjunction with the Wiener Werkstätte between 1904 and 1911, was for a wealthy young Belgian, Adolphe Stoclet. Given carte-blanche to create a sumptuous modern residence on the avenue de Terveuren in the Brussels suburbs, Hoffmann spared nothing in providing a

25

24 Josef M. Olbrich, drawing for *Ver Sacrum* of the Secession exhibition building, Vienna, 1898

showcase for the new Viennese workshops. The result was a formal and austere mansion of square block construction sheathed in marble, accentuated at the angles with embossed copper mouldings. For the interior of the building (which has survived in its original state), Hoffmann deployed the full range of the workshops' design and technical skills. Gustav Klimt's dining-room murals, executed in mosaics of marble, gold and semi-precious gems, set the tone for the lavish effect sought throughout.

The Palais Stoclet proved conclusively that the new movement was not dependent on curves and fanciful ornamentation for its legitimacy. Fine materials and relentless perpendiculars were shown to be as suitable for a dwelling as for a business building.

For late 19th-century traditionalists in Germany, the most vulgar manifestations of the emerging *Jugendstil* movement, and clear proof

25 Josef Hoffmann, dining room of the Palais Stoclet, Brussels, 1904–11, with murals by Gustav Klimt

26 August Endell, façade of the Atelier Elvira, Munich, 1897–98

of its aberrance, were visible in August Endell's Atelier Elvira, a 26 Munich photographic studio (1897–98). Illustrations of the building's façade and interior, widely published in contemporary art magazines, reveal an ill-conceived, if not plainly hideous, asymmetrical design that floats uncertainly and arbitrarily across the façade; some critics sought to link this to *rocaille* antecedents. For most, the problem was the absence of a direct relationship between the fantastic ornamentation and the building, which was conventional in form. Endell's later buildings in the modernist idiom, including his design for the auditorium of the Buntes Theater in Berlin (1901), were far more coherent, but his name will always be associated negatively with his seminal modernist design for the Atelier Elvira.

Jugendstil was fashionable elsewhere in southern Germany, particularly in Darmstadt, where both Olbrich and Behrens applied it conceptually to the houses they designed around 1900 for the

47

Mathildenhöhe colony. Behrens's infatuation with the new move-ment was short-lived, however; by 1904 he abandoned the curve entirely and ultimately became even more severe, in his rejection of any form of architectural ornament, than Adolf Loos in Vienna.

Italy's contribution in architecture to the *Stile Liberty* was limited largely to Raimondo d'Aronco's flamboyant designs for the principal buildings and thoroughfares of the 1902 Turin Exposition site: its entrances, central rotunda, fine arts pavilion, furniture gallery, etc. Several other architects participated in the new movement with spirited renditions inspired in part by the Paris Salons and in part by the Beaux-Arts eclecticism popular in Italy at the time. Of these, Giuseppe Sommaruga's Palazzo Castiglioni in Milan (1903) and Villa Romeo (also in Milan, 1908) expressed the Italians' spontaneous embrace of the latest decorative fad. Elsewhere, a handful of isolated buildings – mostly private residences – bear witness to the *Stile Floreale*'s brief popularity in Italy: Brega's Villa Ruggeri, in Pesaro (1902–07); Bossi's Galimberti house, in Milan (1905); and Michelaz-zi's villino Broggi-Caraceni, in Florence (1911).

Progressive architecture in England around 1900 aligned itself more with the indigenous Arts and Crafts Movement than with developments across the Channel. Forsaking bold or reckless

27 Raimondo d'Aronco, music pavilion at the Turin Exposition, 1902

28 Giovanni Michelazzi, villino Broggi-Caraceni, Florence, 1911

experimentation, and distrustful of anything commercially successful, the nation's avant-garde architectural community settled on a
type of proto-Art Nouveau manner that was eminently reasonable,
moderate and simple, in which the triumphs of revived handcraftsmanship were readily evident.

Voysey, whose building style conveyed the cultivated rustic
quality sought by many of his colleagues, summed up the English
attitude to the European movement in an article in *The Magazine of
Art*, 'Surely *l'Art Nouveau* is not worthy to be called a style. Is it not
merely the work of a lot of imitators with nothing but mad
eccentricity as a guide; good men, no doubt, misled into thinking that
Art is a debauch of sensuous feeling, instead of the expression of
human *thought* and feeling combined, and governed by reverence for
something higher than human nature?' In short, there was no English
Art Nouveau architecture if one centres one's definition around the
works of Horta and Guimard.

To the north, however, Mackintosh electrified the emerging
modernist schools in Austria and Germany with his attempts to revise

the Scottish baronial style. His designs for the Glasgow School of Art (1896–1909), Hill House in Helensburgh (1902–03); four tearooms in Glasgow for a Miss Cranston (between 1897 and 1904), and Windyhill in Kilmacolm (1900–01) reveal his attempt not only to develop a matrix of new architectural concepts, but at the same time to unify the exteriors of his buildings with the decoration on their interiors. Had he restricted his experimentation to the buildings themselves – in particular, to his search for a novel asymmetrical system of massing and fenestration – he would have avoided the antipathy of the English critics (and several Scottish ones, too). His contributions to architecture *per se* were seen as legitimate, especially his ability to create an independent aesthetic value for his architectural elements in the role they played between broken and unbroken surfaces. His choice of a decorative grammar of ornament, however, was perceived widely as unacceptable.

Today, as one examines Mackintosh's surviving interiors, or the renderings of those that were never executed, it is hard to comprehend the genuine outrage they aroused at the time. Certainly some of his decorative motifs can be considered weird or disquieting – particularly the ghost-like visions of attenuated young women with which he adorned some of his friezes and furniture panels (Mackintosh and his three Glaswegian colleagues became known as 'the Spook School' for their repeated use of such imagery) – but the crisp verticality and spatial articulation of his interiors stood in stark refutation of the curved contours and *entrelacs* prevalent on the Continent, and for this he seems never to have received the credit he deserved.

In response to its loss of independence to Spain at the end of the 18th century, Catalonia experienced a revival of cultural and political nationalism in the 1870s. In the vanguard of the separatist movement were Barcelona's leading architects, including Lluis Doménech i Montaner and José Puig i Cadafalch, who expressed their opposition to Spanish rule in their rejection of historic styles.

The search for a new Catalan style of architecture led to Modernismo, a regional re-elaboration known as neo-Mudéjar, which included Moorish decorative forms and techniques, such as tiled surfaces used in contrasting patterns on brick buildings. In 1904, Puig reviewed the recent architectural revolution,

> a modern art based on our own traditional forms, embellishing
> them with the beautiful properties of new materials, finding

29 Charles Rennie Mackintosh,
Buchanan Street tearooms,
Glasgow, 1897

solutions to today's problems through a spirit of nationalism. We
have injected into it something of the decorative exuberance of our
medieval tradition, charged with an almost Moorish flavour and a
certain vaguely Oriental quality. It has been a collective labour by
independent visionaries and their more conservative predecessors
alike – a work of masters and disciples. All this has been helped
along by a literary, social and historical renaissance.

Today, turn-of-the-century Catalan architecture continues to defy
easy categorization, as does that of its brilliant and enigmatic master,
Antoni Gaudí i Cornet. Born of humble origins in or near the market-
town of Reus in Tarragona, Gaudí initially mixed respectable neo-
Gothicism and Modernismo. Towards 1900, however, as in the Casa
Calvet (1898–1904), he increasingly gave evidence of a single-minded
approach that sought to blend ingenious structural solutions with eye-

catching decorative effects. The calm logic of his structures, distinguished by their novel internal systems of bracing and support, is invariably concealed beneath a riot of ornamental colour and a wealth of decorative effects.

Gaudí's truly Art Nouveau structures date from around 1903, at the time when the movement was in retreat in the rest of Europe. His most celebrated buildings – the Casa Batlló (1904–06) and Casa Milà (1906–08) – take on the aspect of living organisms with biomorphic surfaces and undulating walls. In response to the inevitable controversy that erupted over their distorted forms, Gaudí cited in his defence that there are no straight lines in nature. The Park Güell (1900–1914) and the chapel Santa Coloma de Cervelló (1898–1914) further established his reputation as an eccentric genius motivated in part by religious and nationalist fervour. The Sagrada Familia cathedral, Gaudí's most famous structure, reveals the problems of categorization that arise in a review of his architecture. Whereas the lower stages of the façade reveal both Modernismo and naturalist impulses, the building's pinnacles draw their inspiration from Gothic forms.

Art Nouveau-inspired buildings were erected in Barcelona by other architects, notably Domenech, whose designs for the Casa Thomas (1895–98), Casa Lleó Morera (1905), and Palau de la Musica Catalana (1905–08), show a restrained enthusiasm for the new movement. The era belonged entirely to Gaudí, however, and these experiments by his contemporaries seem timid and irrelevant now.

Whereas the development of modernist trends within American architecture towards the turn of the century can in some ways be identified with that in Europe, the parallels remain complex and often obscure. Certainly, Louis Sullivan's choice of a highly condensed and luxuriant vegetal grammar of ornament with which to dress his new buildings bears close comparison with the work of Guimard, Sommaruga and others on the Continent, yet it was applied in most part to tall commercial buildings of classical form. Unadorned, these structures do not qualify as Art Nouveau, even though their lower reaches are covered with an exquisite skein of colourful foliage rendered in low relief. The ornamentation therefore appears detached, an issue which Nikolaus Pevsner addressed in his discussion in *The Sources of Modern Architecture and Design* of Sullivan's Guaranty Building (1894-95), 'In technique and in its strong vertical emphasis it points towards the twentieth century, but its elaborate and complex ornament places it still in the age of Art Nouveau.'

52

31 Louis Sullivan, detail of cast iron work on the Carson, Pirie, Scott department store, Chicago, 1899–1904

The same criticism may be applied to other Sullivan buildings, including the Wainwright (St. Louis, 1890–91), Schiller (1891–93), Bayard (New York, 1897–98), Chicago Stock Exchange (1893–94) and the Carson, Pirie, Scott department store in Chicago (1899–1904). In his choice of texture, pattern and colour, Sullivan qualified as an exponent of Art Nouveau; in the strictly traditional massing of his buildings, he did not. An appropriate comment was made by the critic H. W. Desmond in his review in *Architectural Record* of the completion of the Carson, Pirie, Scott store in 1904,

> For, let it be well understood, Mr. Sullivan is our only Modernist. He is, moreover, strictly of our soil . . . the first American architect. To say that he has invented a style would, of course, be to say too much, but he has certainly evolved and elaborated a highly artistic form of superficial decorative expression in logical connection with the American steel skeleton building . . . Here is L'Art Nouveau indigenous to the United States, nurtured upon American problems . . .

Beyond Sullivan, no other American architect bears consideration within an Art Nouveau context. Whereas others developed exciting new architectural forms – most notably, Frank Lloyd Wright and Greene & Greene in their Prairie School and Bungalow styles – their work is now seen as part of the Arts and Crafts movement.

54

CHAPTER THREE

Furniture

In the course of the 19th century, European furniture makers, and especially those in France, fell into the practice of rehashing earlier styles, sometimes mixing one period of the great 18th-century *ébénistes* with another. In other words, one could find a Louis XIV Boulle commode on tapering cylindrical Louis XVI feet enhanced with Louis XV ormolu *sabots*. The style was wryly called 'all the Louis', and critics inveighed against the lack of creativity that nurtured it. For example, Michel Chevalier, director of the International Jury at the 1867 Exposition Universelle in Paris wrote, 'from the surviving monuments of our art, future historians will take us to be a fantastic people, living partially in the Greek tradition, partly in that of the Italian Renaissance, and partly as 18th-century Bourbons, but never having had a life of our own.'

In Europe as a whole, the situation was more or less the same. Only Biedermeier, introduced in Germany and Austria around 1815, provided a brief moment of innovation, though it was a direct and rather obvious classical clone. Victorian furniture in Great Britain was addicted to ornamentation: chairs and desks adorned with elaborately pierced crest-rails and frieze drawers, often with a strong Oriental or Hispano-Moresque influence, amid suffocatingly cluttered interiors.

Dissatisfaction with these mainstream tendencies was voiced largely by architects, who provided the early impetus for change. Not only were whiplash organic contours introduced onto the façades of buildings, as we have seen, but entire interiors were designed to match. The beginnings of a fruitful cooperation among artists of various kinds were recognized most clearly by the architect and art critic Francis Jourdain, who wrote in an 1899 article on modern furniture in *La Revue d'art*, 'It is a time when the architect walks hand in hand with the artist, sculptor, engraver, musician, man of letters and the decorator. All have an identical vision, a common aesthetic goal and a single ideal.'

As far as the French went, the main criticism of the Art Nouveau grammar of ornament was that it violated the nation's proud heritage

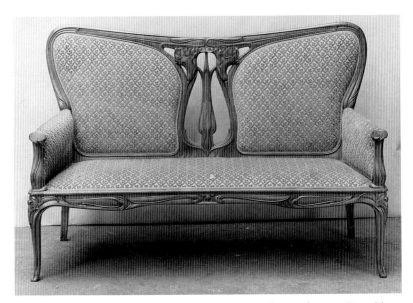

32 Georges de Feure, a canapé exhibited in Bing's pavilion at the 1900 Exposition Universelle

in furniture. A fundamental problem was that it offended against the basic laws of cabinetmaking: a piece of furniture had primarily to be well-constructed and functional; only then did one set about decorating it. Turn-of-the-century designers put the emphasis on the decoration. At its apogee, an Art Nouveau piece of furniture might resemble a flowering bush or tree; its feet were transformed into roots, its framework into the trunk and main branches, and its cornice into blossoms. If this were not enough, various entomological horrors – beetles, dragonflies and bugs – became drawer pulls or random sculpted decoration. Purists railed at the worst excesses of Art Nouveau designs, ignoring the quieter masterpieces by Louis Majorelle, Eugène Gaillard, Victor Horta and many others, which fell well within traditional limits.

Fortunately, not all the commentary was negative, nor was it aimed at all Art Nouveau furniture designers. The critic G. M. Jacques, who had referred earlier to the new art's 'reign of terror', 32 found Georges de Feure's furniture at the 1900 Exposition Universelle delightful:

> de Feure's exhibit characterizes perfectly the spirit of Bing's shop. It is not the work of a revolutionary; it is not a question of overthrowing everything or of turning everything upside down,

33 Emile Gallé, dragonfly table, c. 1898

of exterminating the legitimate past and of eliminating the rules of geometry. It is, on the contrary, a true return to nature of which the first innovators, hot-headed in their impetuosity to destroy, had lost their vision. Each piece of de Feure's furniture is, above all, a good, honest and unpretentious work of cabinetry.

In Paris, Bing and Meier-Graefe, both having galleries devoted to Art Nouveau, were ardent publicists; and certain critics – in particular Gustave Soulier – promoted the new art in their coverage of the annual Salons. In his hometown, Nancy, Gallé generated an abundant stream of written and spoken words to promote the cause of using nature as embellishment. Other enthusiasts were the Goncourt brothers, Roger Marx and Emile Nicolas, all noted art critics born in Lorraine. In the rest of Europe, comment was more restrained. The foreign critics who covered the Paris Salons and international expositions – especially those for *The Studio* and *Deutsche Kunst und Dekoration* – spent more time bemoaning their countrymen's inabilities than in finding fault elsewhere.

One of the accomplishments of the Art Nouveau era was the concept of the furniture *ensemblier*. Prior to 1900, pieces tended to be designed individually, to fit willy-nilly into the general disharmony of a 19th-century home. Whereas seat furniture was likely to be *en suite*, one had to search separately for the tables, plant stands and vitrines that completed the drawing-room. No common theme unified an interior: period rooms in the Bethnal Green Museum, London, and the Metropolitan Museum of Art, New York, show that eclecticism was the norm. The Art Nouveau philosophy of integrated design brought a definitive change; a room had to be planned in its entirety, and furniture designers were thus forced to show much greater diversity.

By 1905, as the brilliance of the *fin de siècle* dimmed, life returned to its humdrum normalcy. The bourgeoisie had suffered a fall in its standard of living; less disposable income in the average home required a range of cheaper mass-produced furnishings, a challenge immediately met by designers in Germany, Austria and the Low Countries. French cabinetmakers were reluctant to face the prospect of lowered standards, and allowed their northern neighbours to make inroads into the domestic market. In late 1902, the Chambre Syndicate de l'Ameublement staged its first Salon des Industries du Mobilier at the Grand Palais in Paris, with a threefold aim: to boost the local furniture industry in the Faubourg Saint-Antoine, to change

34 Jacques Gruber, cabinet, with veneered and etched glass decoration, c. 1902

French taste, and to combat the progress made by foreign furniture retailers. Incorporated into the Salon was a competition for cheap furniture, in which national manufacturers were invited to participate. Many Art Nouveau exponents responded, among them Mathieu Gallerey, Georges de Feure, Henri Rapin and Théodore Lambert. Lively carved floral panels on rectangular frames replaced the lavish mouldings and sculpted decoration of five years earlier; the emphasis had shifted and economy was the new watchword.

In France, the design and production of Art Nouveau furniture were dominated by the School of Nancy. It is astonishing that such an abundance of cabinetmaking talent could have accumulated in a provincial town in a single, short-lived epoch. The principal exponents were Majorelle, Gallé, Jacques Gruber, Eugène Vallin and, a generation younger, Camille Gauthier, Henri Hamm, Louis Hestaux, Laurent Neiss and Justin Férez. To these must be added the Art Nouveau architect Emile André, who designed a delightful range of furnishings to complement the exterior of his buildings.

33,34

59

Assistance with designs and technical counsel were provided by the ubiquitous Victor Prouvé, and a host of other artisans could be counted on for ancillary furniture materials: Alfred Finot, Ernest Bussière and Ernest Wittmann (sculpted ornamentation); Charles Fridrich and Fernand Courteix (fabrics and textiles); the Daum *frères* (glass); and Lombard (leather).

The main characteristic of Art Nouveau furniture produced in Nancy is the use of nature – most specifically, the flower and its components – as its central decorative theme. Nowhere else was such a realistic interpretation attempted. In Paris, the plant was abstracted and refined; in Germany and Austria its influence was further removed, if not absent.

The undisputed master of Art Nouveau furniture was Louis Majorelle. This judgment was expressed by contemporary critics and today, with the perspective that time affords, it is even more evident. Blessed with superb design sense and technical virtuosity, he was simultaneously artist and artisan, designer and technician. His most fertile years were from 1898 to 1908, when piece after piece of breathtaking quality came onto the market. Few more exquisite 35 pieces have been created at any time than his 1903 desk *aux orchidées* in amaranth and purpleheart with twin corolla glass shades manufactured by the Daum glassworks. Equally spectacular and graceful was the longcase clock which he exhibited in 1901. Many of his masterpieces challenged the works of the great 18th-century cabinet-makers. After 1908, however, the standard dropped sharply, if not precipitously. A decision was taken to industrialize the workshops, and that put an end to extravagance. Gone were the boldness and luxuriance of his ormolu *nénufar* and *orchidée* mounts; in their place a wide range of lightly sculpted furniture for the public at large.

It was as early as 1885 that Gallé added a cabinetmaking and marquetry atelier to his glassworks, thus marking the beginning of a commercial operation which continued long after his death in 1904. In 1894 the workshop was industrialized, allowing the mechanization of various stages of production, as in his glassware. Daily output allowed for small pieces such as tea-tables, screens, *sellettes*, nests of tables and *guéridons*. Only in the 1890s did larger furniture begin to appear: *étagères*, vitrines and entire *ensembles*. Later pieces, those shown from 1900, were infinitely more sophisticated, a reminder that Gallé began his furniture production long after his involvement in glass (*c.* 1874), and that it did not develop simultaneously to the same stage of perfection. His 1904 *Aube et crépuscule* bed – virtually the last

35 Louis Majorelle, desk *aux orchidées*, 1903

piece of furniture he designed – showed that he was on the threshold of a new and important phase in his furniture design at the time of his death.

Unlike Nancy, Paris did not have its own school or principal group. The city was simply too large and diverse to be dominated by a single theme in the decorative arts. Most Art Nouveau exponents, however, operated within loosely defined limits of style; the Salons kept them in touch with prevailing fashions. Only Carabin and Guimard kicked over convention's traces entirely.

41
38

Contemporary art reviews give surprising evidence of the large number of cabinetmakers in the French capital who either regularly or intermittently designed Art Nouveau furniture. The number is close to fifty, indicating to what extent the movement pervaded Paris between 1895 and 1905. Among the designers were Eugène Belville, Albert Angst, Léon Benouville, Louis Bigaux, Joseph Boverie, Rupert Carabin, Edouard Colonna, Georges de Feure, Eugène Gaillard, Hector Guimard, Théodore Lambert, Abel Landry, Georges Nowak, Charles Plumet and Tony Selmersheim, Pierre Selmersheim, Henri Sauvage, and many more, besides the commercial firm of Diot, which manufactured a wide range of *genre* pieces.

36–40

36 Léon Benouville,
corner of a salon,
c. 1902

37 Abel Landry, chair
designed for La Maison
Moderne, 1901

38 Hector Guimard,
armchair, pearwood,
c. 1902

39 Eugène Gaillard, hall *étagère*, in collaboration with Paul-Emile Mangeant, *c.* 1902

40 Edouard Colonna, tea table, *c.* 1900

41 Rupert Carabin, sketch for the walnut table, *fauteuil* and *chaise* exhibited at the Société Nationale des Beaux-Arts, 1896

For many of these, the annual Salons afforded an incomparable opportunity to display their latest works. In fact, the Salons became *de rigueur*: the critics seldom strayed beyond the Champs-de-Mars or the Grand Palais, and their published opinions could dictate success or oblivion. Other important stepping-stones in the careers of Art Nouveau furniture designers were Bing's Maison Art Nouveau and Meier-Graefe's La Maison Moderne, the exhibitions of L'Art dans Tout (formerly Les Cinq and then Les Six), and, of course, the 1900 Exposition Universelle.

In Brussels, the momentum for Art Nouveau furniture was provided by the city's architects. As J.-G.-G. Watelet noted in *Discovering Antiques* in 1971, 'The main characteristic of Belgian furniture of this period is its architectural quality, which shows itself in two different ways. First of all, most of the furniture was designed to fit in with a particular architectural scheme and it does not often stand on its own merits . . . second, furniture of this period can be called architectural because it is mainly the work of architects.' Three people predominated: Horta, van de Velde and Serrurier-Bovy, all of whom designed total interiors in harmony with their buildings. Others who deserve brief mention were Paul Hankar, Georges Hobé, Antoine Pompe and Georges Lemmen, all of them exhibitors at the Salons of Les Vingt. The tapestry weaver, Edouard de Grauw, also designed Art Nouveau-inspired furniture in collaboration with the interior designer François König.

Primarily a designer of residential buildings, Horta first had to persuade his clients to let him abandon tradition, not only in the shape and decoration of the house, but in its furnishings. His highly   43
distinctive architectural line was echoed in his furniture, though never with the free reign afforded it in ceiling struts, column capitals and chandeliers. Horta's furniture designs were unique for each client; each commission posed new challenges that required new solutions. None of his designs was made to be reproduced commercially.

Gustave Serrurier-Bovy, the eldest child of a furniture retailer,   44
established his architectural and furniture-manufacturing business at 38 rue de l'Université in Liège. He received an early commission, in 1887, for a university hospital. Others soon followed, but it was not until 1894, when he exhibited a *chambre d'artisan* at the first Salon of La Libre Esthétique, that he launched his career as a decorator. The *ensemble* was characteristic of his later work; brightly coloured ceilings and walls offset the provincial plainness of the furniture. These pieces combined a rustic solidity with pleasant Art Nouveau

42 Charles Rennie Mackintosh, armchair, stained wood and glass, *c.* 1904

curves. Serrurier-Bovy's philosophy remained unchanged for many years: a room's charm lay for him in its perimeter – wallpapers *au pochoir*, painted floral curtains, faience chimney tiles, panelled wainscots, stained-glass windows and curtains. His favourite themes, repeated in each medium, were the carrot, umbel and mimosa. The surface of the furniture, however, remained undecorated, no doubt to avoid clashing with its colourful surroundings.

Henry van de Velde came to the applied arts and architecture as an accomplished Impressionist and Pointillist painter. Never timid about expressing his opinion, he castigated the eclecticism of 19th-century interiors in his *Formule d'une Esthétique Moderne*: 'the insane follies which the furniture makers of past centuries had piled up in bedrooms and drawing-rooms . . . processions of fauns, menacing apocalyptic beasts, benevolently hilarious cupids (bawdy in some cases and complaisantly anxious in others), and swollen-cheeked satyrs in charge of the winds.' To remedy this, he placed emphasis on the interplay of curved lines and empty spaces. Early furniture essays, such as those for his own home, villa Bloemenwerf in Uccle, had a medieval logic and solidity, despite their flowing lines.

A selection of van de Velde's early furniture was illustrated in an exhaustive article in the first issue of *L'Art Décoratif* in 1898. Chairs

43 Victor Horta, bronze door handle on a Horta cupboard, late 1890s

44 Gustav Serrurier-Bovy, bedroom ensemble, *c.* 1902

upholstered in tapestry to his own designs, a stained-glass firescreen, a toiletry table, bookcase, minister's desk, divan with William Morris chintz fabric, and a selection of pieces for Bing, show a restrained Art Nouveau influence, especially in the feet of his chairs, where an occasional whiplash or volute anticipated his later, more mature, 1900 style.

Germany was the first country in the late 1800s to face squarely the consequences of the machine and its inevitable offspring, mass-production. Awareness of the machine's impact on design and, more particularly, of its decorative limitations – i.e., its inability to duplicate the sculpted and veneered decoration of a skilled wood-carver and marqueteur – turned many designers away from the prevailing floral ornateness of French and Belgian furniture. The search was for a viable alternative: design in which function, rather than superficial decoration, might be the criterion of beauty. Contemporary issues of *Innendekoration* and *Kunst und Kunsthandwerk* give evidence that German designers did not respond to the Art Nouveau idiom with either the enthusiasm or spontaneity of their neighbours. In fact, the

67

45 Peter Behrens, dining room chair, oak, 1902

exceptions went overboard: the few truly *Jugendstil* pieces of furniture by August Endell, Peter Behrens and Bernhard Pankok, for example, appear overly exuberant, if not undisciplined, when compared with the forms of their colleagues in the Munich Secession. The critic for *The Studio* noted correctly, in 1901, that 'there is more sobriety, more judgement in the decoration of the Secessionist galleries than in French furniture.'

Notwithstanding the general absence of Art Nouveau influence, several pieces of furniture by German designers merit mention. In Bavaria, Richard Riemerschmid designed a range of furniture, mainly chairs, in the new idiom. Quiet and rational shapes borrow an

46 August Endell,
armchair, 1899

occasional volute or scroll from the Art Nouveau vocabulary. Also in
Munich, Pankok designed various pieces with a lightly pronounced
Art Nouveau flavour, as did Hermann Obrist, whose designs (like
those of Pankok and Bruno Paul) were executed by the Vereinigte
Werkstätte für Kunst im Handwerk.

Peter Behrens, the professor of architecture who included among
his students the illustrious triad of Gropius, van der Rohe and Le
Corbusier, designed a select number of pieces of somewhat unconventional furniture, including those for his house in the Mathildenhöhe colony in Darmstadt. Other examples of his furniture, such as
the chairs in the vestibule he designed for the German pavilion at the

45

1902 Turin Exposition, imparted a feeling of organic restraint, in line with the German designers' reluctance to fall in with France's fleeting infatuation with the new movement.

Several other designers flirted with Art Nouveau, among them 46 August Endell, who created open armchairs with sculpted finials and capitals that recall pieces made by Hector Guimard for the Castel Béranger. Otto Eckmann, a member of the Munich Secession, and Patriz Huber in Darmstadt preferred a more rigorous Arts and Crafts approach, while Albin Müller, in Dresden, applied *Jugendstil* floral and scrolled brass key plates and door hinges to rectilinear structures. Also in Dresden were Otto Fischer, Johann Cissarz, Professor Karl Gross and E. Schaudt. In Düsseldorf, Professor G. Oeder designed a range of Art Nouveau furniture, while in Leipzig F. A. Schütz included similar modernist editions in his sales catalogues.

Despite his training as an architect, the Scotsman Charles Rennie Mackintosh is better known today as a designer of furniture or, more specifically, of chairs. This is ironic, as his furnishings were initially a natural and secondary corollary of his buildings; they were designed to delineate the interior spaces in which his clients would spend most of their time.

In 1896, Mackintosh collaborated with George Walton on the interior of Miss Cranston's Tea-Rooms in Buchanan Street, Glasgow. Although the young Mackintosh was Walton's assistant in the project, it was his style and flair that delighted Miss Cranston and which led to his independent commission for her Argyle Street Tea-Rooms the following year. In his first major commission to combine architecture and furniture design, all the pieces – chairs, settees, benches, card- and domino-tables and umbrella stands – are characterized by bold outlines and box-line shapes. The architectonic features of his later designs had already matured. Tall, slender back-42 rests with ladderback splats or pierced oval crests match the soaring linear contours of his buildings. Mackintosh's wood of choice was oak, its rich grain heightened with a clear varnish or, later, as at the Turin Exposition, painted white.

Mackintosh's private commissions proliferated after 1897. Among them were the Ingram Street Tea-Rooms and Main Street flat in 1900; Westel, in Queen's Place, in 1901; the Wärndorfer Musik Salon, Vienna, and the Hill House, Helensburgh, in 1902; Hous' Hill in 1903; and the Willow Tea-Rooms in 1904. For these, Mackintosh is believed to have designed well over four hundred objects, from chairs to cutlery and cruet sets, with the same intricacy and care.

Also in Glasgow, the firm of Wylie & Lochhead manufactured a wide range of furniture for the middle class. Today identifiable as stylistically midway between Art Nouveau and Arts and Crafts – it drew inspiration from both, in fact – the firm's design department was overseen by Ernest Archibald Taylor, George Logan and John Ednie. Two other Glaswegian designers of note, Herbert MacNair and George Walton, created a small amount of modernist furniture; but they inevitably felt overshadowed by the genius of Mackintosh and both left Glasgow in 1898.

In England, William Morris's apostles did not pursue the natural evolution of his teachings into turn-of-the-century modernism, as did the Glasgow School and Vienna. English furniture makers around 1900 clung to vaguely 18th-century forms enhanced with the newly fashionable Arts and Crafts motifs. None of the London artist-designers who became prominent in other areas of Art Nouveau design – in particular, Ashbee and Voysey – advanced their furniture designs beyond a sturdy Burges- or Morris-like form; not appreciably different, in fact, from the pieces manufactured by the Guild of Handicraft and the Art Workers' Guild in the 1890s. The earlier chair and cabinet by Mackmurdo, which in its free forms and plant motifs clearly anticipated an English participation in the European Art Nouveau movement, found no later adherents.

The initial Viennese Secessionist style took its inspiration from Mackintosh's architectural and furniture designs. Whereas the Glaswegian's elongated linear style was highly popular, the Secessionists soon rejected his heavy decorative imagery – the symbolist rose and attentuated virginal maidens – in favour of their own stark and achromatic forms of ornamentation.

Leading the search in Austria for a new national decorative identity was Josef Hoffmann, whose furniture designs were executed from 1903 through the bentwood furniture manufacturers, Kohn and Thonet. Hoffmann's earlier designs, illustrated in a 1901 essay 'Simple Furniture', reveal Mackintosh's influence, but Hoffmann's functionalism eventually superseded the Scot's aestheticism. A.S. Levetus wrote in 1906 of Hoffmann's furniture, 'utility is the first condition, but there is no reason why the simplest articles should not be beautiful. The value does not lie only in the material, but in the right thought and treatment of the material, and its power to convey that thought to the minds of others . . .'

Two of Hoffmann's most important interior design commissions generated some of his finest furniture. The first was the Purkersdorf

47 Koloman Moser, armchair, rosewood, maple and mother-of-pearl, 1904

48 Otto Wagner, chair, bent beechwood, plywood and aluminium, *c.* 1903

sanatorium, near Vienna, in 1904–05, for which he created a variety of elegant side- and dining-chairs with pierced oval back-rests and splats. The second, in 1907, was the Kabarett Fledermaus, a favourite rendezvous of fashionable Vienna. Here, Hoffmann's designs for the interior were dazzlingly neat and uncluttered; utilitarian tables and chairs with ball joints were painted in spartan black and white. Opening with Oskar Kokoschka's *The Spotted Egg*, the playhouse was soon frequented more by design students than theatre buffs. The chairs are classics of 20th-century design.

49

Closely associated with Hoffmann, Koloman Moser was an artist turned designer. His furniture, mostly executed by Kohn, included a dining-room suite in mahogany and sycamore inlaid with brass, and beechwood chairs painted white and with aluminium shoes. Smaller items, such as his stepped square metal plant-stands and candlesticks, are often indistinguishable from those of Hoffmann. Among the others who adopted the distinctive Wiener Werkstätte brand of modernism in their furniture designs were Otto Wagner, Josef M. Olbrich and Adolf Loos.

47

48

72

49 Josef Hoffmann, side chair for Kabarett Fledermaus, 1907

The furniture designs of Antoni Gaudí were limited to the interiors of his own buildings. Although most pieces were made of rough-hewn oak, they bear the eccentric stamp of his genius. In 1878, the year he met his future patron Eusebio Güell y Bacigalupi, Gaudí created his first piece of furniture: a desk for himself. A curious baroque structure with curved cupboards and twin pedestal drawers raised on spindly feet, it anticipated his future break with convention.

Gaudí's architectural flair assured him an abundance of commissions. In 1885 he began his design for Güell's house in the calle Conda de Asalto, Barcelona. The furnishings included an odd kidney-shaped *chaise longue* with tufted upholstery, inspired by the cross-section of a chambered nautilus shell, and a dressing table, both of which defy easy stylistic categorization. A chair with padded armrests terminating in carved dragons showed that he adhered for some time to conventional concepts of furniture design; it was only in 1898, when he began work on the Casa Calvet, that a complete divorce from tradition became evident. The oak chairs and benches have shield-shaped backs

50

50 Antoni Gaudí, oak bench for Casa Calvet, 1898–1904

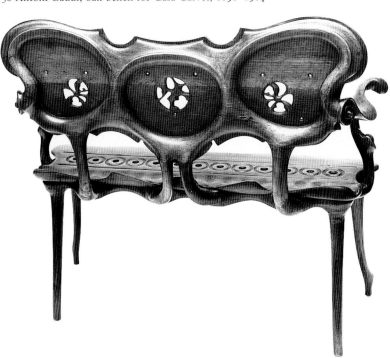

51 Gaspar Homar, double bed and night table, mahogany with veneered panels, *c.* 1904

pierced with trefoil leaf motifs. There is a cavalier Guimard defiance to their free forms and a Mackintosh disregard for their rudimentary finish. Gaudí's *prie-dieux* for the chapel of the Colona Güell, begun in the same year, incorporated the same combination of visionary design and rigorous woodwork. In 1906 came his designs for the Casa Battló. The chairs, designed as double- and seven-seated units, were angled variations on the Casa Calvet models.

Apart from Gaudí, only three other Catalan designers turned their energies to Art Nouveau furniture: Alejo Clapés Puig, Gaspar Homar and Juan Busquets.

As in Spain, Italian Art Nouveau furniture was dominated by a single man, Carlo Bugatti, who was described by the critic Maxime LeRoy in 1903 as 'an isolated genius whose flair for the bizarre defies classification'. Bugatti's interpetation of the new art was, in fact, unique, drawing on a marvellous mix of Hispano-Moresque architectural influences painted with Japanese bamboo shoots and other exotic details. Pseudo-Arabic minarets, dentils and spindled galleries silhouette the outlines of furniture designed on the circle and its parts – the arc and chord. The wooden frame was covered in chamois leather within *repoussé* metal mounts or veneered in pewter and brass with insect-like motifs and Middle Eastern calligraphy. Tassels, either singly or in fringes, added to the theatrical effect. The critics were variously perplexed, excited or outraged.

Bugatti's furniture for the Turin Exposition was sharply different from his earlier creations. His 'Snail' room, one of four *ensembles* displayed, emphasized the striking modernity of his new furniture; the unbroken sweep from their pierced circular back-rests down, and

53

52 Carlo Zen, desk, wood inlaid with mother-of-pearl and with ormolu mounts, *c.* 1905

53 Carlo Bugatti, psyche mirror, inlaid satinwood, *c.* 1900

through, their short feet to the flat circular seat resembled an upended snail. The pale beige vellum covering appears, at first glance, to be plastic, giving the impression that the chairs were made of injection-moulded plastic, a commercial reality that came to maturity fifty years later.

No one else in Italy tried to match Bugatti's idiosyncratic genius. Eugenio Quarti, a fellow Milanese and close friend, adopted a restrained Art Nouveau type of furniture design based on the Parisian volute. Another cabinetmaker, Carlo Zen, used a florid and curvaceous brand of Art Nouveau in the furniture which he showed at the expositions of the time.

It is one of the curiosities of Art Nouveau's short history that whereas American artists and craftsmen made a significant contribution to the movement in various other fields – particularly glassware and ceramics – it was never embraced by furniture designers in the United States.

CHAPTER FOUR

Painting and the Graphic Arts

Since the impact of Art Nouveau on the fine arts was ambiguous and often only peripheral, it is harder to define than in other disciplines. The movement was largely a way of *designing*, rather than painting *per se*, and was therefore more readily expressed by plastic treatment than on a flat surface. Yet many of Art Nouveau's principal elements – for example, the simplification of form, the flattening of space, the evocative power of the undulating line and its affinity for symbolism – were in some ways anticipated on canvas and paper before they were adopted in the applied arts. Nevertheless, if there was no Art Nouveau school of painting as such (and most art historians maintain there was not), the movement was so encompassing that it had a decided effect on a substantial number of artists who came to maturity in the 1890s, irrespective of the direction their work ultimately took.

In the early 1880s, Impressionism was challenged on several fronts by groups aspiring to the new avant-garde, all in reaction against the illusionistic conception of form and the resulting dissolution of surface and line. Two new societies, Les Vingt in Brussels and the Société des Artistes Indépendants in Paris, both exerted an immense influence on Post-Impressionist art. Led by the French, all the main schools of late 19th- and early 20th-century European painting – the Symbolists, the English Pre-Raphaelites, the German Expressionists, the Nabis and the Fauves – used elements of space, colour, imagery and composition that were also used by the exponents of Art Nouveau. In general, however, painting in the Art Nouveau movement fell far short of these schools; though often highly decorative, it lacked intellectual content. Nevertheless, a brief review of some of the pre-eminent artists and schools of the period will reveal the degree to which one or more of the leading tendencies of the Art Nouveau movement affected the work of all progressive artists, whatever their particular stylistic affiliation or intellectual orientation.

Paul Gauguin provides a typical example. Returning in 1888 from a 54 stay in Martinique, he settled in Pont-Aven, in Brittany, where he could work in relative isolation, immune to developments in Paris. Gauguin's belief that ideas and emotional experiences could be suggested on canvas by equivalents in colour and line led to the style of painting known from 1890 as Symbolism, in which many of the most important components of Art Nouveau were evident: in particular, the use of bold abstract outlines and the abandonment of natural colours and colour harmonies. Gauguin also eliminated perspective and reduced the depth of his compositions to a flat plane on which images were applied in rhythmic patterns, reminding us yet again of the pervasive influence of *Japonisme* on the European art of the age. By these means, he sought to suspend the definition of the object in order to express its purely decorative value in two-dimensional terms. Gauguin was joined by Emile Bernard and, later, by Paul Sérusier, for whom the purpose of art was 'the evolution of an idea without expressing it'.

Sérusier, in turn, was a founding member of the group who called themselves the Nabis ('Prophets'). They included Denis, Bonnard, Ibels and Ranson, who were soon joined by Vuillard, Roussel, Séguin and Vallotton. Denis described the group's goal: 'a picture – before

54 Paul Gauguin, *Aha oe feii? (What, are you jealous?)*, oil on canvas, 1892

55 Paul and France Ranson, folding screen, silk embroidery with stencilled designs, c. 1892

being a battle horse, a female nude or some anecdote – is essentially a flat surface covered with colours assembled in a certain order.' The Nabis' belief in the primacy of the flat surface allowed them to expand their interest beyond the painter's canvas to other two-dimensional media, including screens, stained glass windows, posters, mosaics and stage sets, examples of which were crafted within the Pont-Aven community. The history of this integration of the fine and applied arts by the Nabis was recalled in 1923 by one of its members, Jan Verkade, 'About the beginning of the year 1890, a war cry was issued from one studio to the other. No more easel paintings! Down with these useless objects! Painting must not usurp the freedom which isolates it from the other arts . . . there are no paintings, there are only decorations.' Here, again, a cornerstone of the Art Nouveau philosophy – the total artistic environment – was embraced eagerly by another group.

The paintings of Odilon Redon likewise reveal certain Art Nouveau sympathies. On intimate terms with the Symbolist poets, and like them drawing on the dream world for his inspiration, Redon created compositions on the frontier of reality and fantasy. To achieve the desired contrasts, he introduced black as an essential colour and used distinct contours to establish the forms in his compositions.

Less evident, but equally important, was the impact of the pointillist Georges Seurat, who exhibited his masterpiece, *The Bathers*, at the Salon des Indépendants in 1884. Seurat's application of a linear composition to his pictures made the viewer aware of their deliberate construction, in contrast to the Impressionists, who had sought an effect of verisimilitude. Perhaps more important and direct, in an Art Nouveau context, was Seurat's influence on the three young Belgian members of Les Vingt, van de Velde, Lemmen and van Rysselberghe, all of whom later forsook painting for the applied arts. More than the other two, it was van de Velde who promoted an abstract vocabulary of Art Nouveau ornament, both in his designs in a variety of media and in his writings. His images, which depict fluid organisms derived from plant life, often set in an ambiguous space, evoke in the viewer a symbolist rather than literal response.

Another exhibitor at Les Vingt, the Dutch artist Jan Toorop, was a friend of the Symbolist poet, Maurice Maeterlinck, who had inspired him to work in a Symbolist style. Toorop's drawings of the early 1890s, such as *The Three Brides*, project a mood of sadness and mystery that achieves an elaborate literary metaphor. Today, however, such compositions appear too haunting and sentimental, and less successful in an Art Nouveau context than his seemingly guileless depictions of young women. In these – for example, *The Girl with the Swans* (1892) – Toorop embraced a rich and nervous curvilinear imagery in which the maidens' long hair was transformed into an rhythmic play of parallel lines with a rich decorative value of its own. Toorop had grown up in Indonesia, in the Dutch East Indies, and brought to his mature style the influence of Javanese batiks and shadow puppets.

Another Dutch artist, Jan Thorn-Prikker, produced a similar range of paintings. His emphasis was on religious symbolism, as in *The Bride* (1892), where clear definition yielded to images and patterns implied by sweeping curved lines and enveloping shapes.

The British influence on Belgian and Dutch painters during the 1880s and '90s was significant, in part because artists such as Whistler and Beardsley had been invited to participate at Les Vingt since its inception. The Pre-Raphaelite Edward Burne-Jones exerted a parti-

56

56 Jan Thorn-Prikker, *The Bride*, oil on canvas, 1892

cular influence in his use of elaborate surface design and in his choice of subject-matter – often gentle young women of melancholic or meditative countenance rendered in a soft palette. Burne-Jones's influence, as well as that of the French Symbolist Gustave Moreau, is evident in the work of the Belgian artist, Ferdinand Khnopff, who was of English descent and who emerged as Belgium's foremost Symbolist. Like Toorop, Khnopff was associated with Maeterlinck, whose poetic imagery is often paralleled in his paintings.

59 In 1900, Vienna could boast of one, if not the quintessential, Art Nouveau artist: Gustav Klimt. Certainly no other artist's work embodied the movement more fully in terms of such issues as the art of surface decoration, flowing curves and rich ornamentation, ephemeral beauty and symbolic feminine imagery tinged with decadence. Klimt is best known for his allegorical portraits of voluptuous young women set against sumptuously textured backgrounds. His use of appliqués, such as sequins, probably inspired by Byzantine mosaics, in some ways anticipated today's collage. Like the Nabis, Klimt moved easily from canvas to other surfaces, creating between 1900 and 1903 large murals for three faculties at the University of Vienna, which were greeted at their unveiling with severe censure because of the radical character of their symbolism. His landscapes and floral compositions, rendered in a kaleidoscopic and compact curvilinear imagery, mixed representational elements with freely invented geometric ornaments.

The Norwegian Edvard Munch was probably the most gifted and intellectual artist who worked in the Art Nouveau idiom. He expressed his philosophy in 1889, in what would soon seem like an understatement of his acute sensitivity to life's hardships, 'No longer should interiors be painted, with people reading and women knitting. They should be living people who breathe and feel, suffer and love.' Munch's paintings convey the *fin-de-siècle* general mood of pessimism with a minimum of descriptive or narrative elements. The critic Peter Selz has described the full impact of Munch's most celebrated work,

57 *The Cry* (1893):

A writhing figure emerges from the picture plane, and its convoluted form is repeated throughout the landscape in the sinuous line of the shore and the equivalent rhythm of the clouds. The curved line is strongly emphasized by its contrast to the straight, rapid diagonal cutting through the imaginary space of the painting. The cry that the central figure seems to be uttering

57 Edvard Munch, *The Cry*, oil on board, 1893

pervades the landscape like a stone creating centrifugal ripples in water. Munch has painted what might be called sound waves, and these lines make the human figure merge with the landscape to express a total anxiety that evokes an immediate response from the observer.

Certainly, no other Art Nouveau artist applied its principal themes – particularly the all-important line – with such intellectual impact. In his hands, the line became a genuine expression of deep psychological involvement.

The Graphic Arts

Art Nouveau was far more successful in its application to the various disciplines within the graphic arts – posters, woodcuts, illustrated books and typography – than to the realm of painting. Its contribution to poster art, in particular, was phenomenal.

As the formal language of Art Nouveau developed in the 1880s, it naturally found expression in the poster, as in everything else. Yet it is important to note that some of this language had actually been drawn from the field of poster art, where it had long been evident. Thus there was an interdependence and easy alliance between the Art Nouveau movement and the poster world, in which both clearly owed a great debt to an earlier influence: the Japanese printmaker.

One of the significant ways that poster art differs from painting is that the poster needs to be viewed in contrast to everything around it, such as fleetingly on a billboard seen from the street. It requires distinct images and a large and succinct written message. In order to maximize its impact, a special artistic methodology evolved for the poster, consisting of strong colour harmonies, vibrant linear rhythms, silhouetted images and the subtle integration of the lettering into the composition as a whole.

In France, the art of the poster was well established by the late 1880s, in large part due to Jules Chéret, a pioneer in the medium, who had opened his lithography workshop in Paris as early as 1866. Chéret was well-placed at the advent of Art Nouveau, and produced many of his more than 1,000 recorded poster designs in the modern style in the promotion of such consumer products as Saxoleine combustion fuel, Job cigarette papers and Dubonnet. Chéret's mastery of the medium is evident in his dynamic use of typography and his isolation of images. Sadly, few of Chéret's posters have survived: designed for

58

58 Jules Chéret, *Fleur de Lotus*, poster for the Folies Bergère, 1893

billboards, most of them were torn down and replaced within a week or two of their first appearance.

The Nabis applied the same theories of picture construction to their graphic art as to their canvases: images were simplified, perspectives were eliminated, colours were flattened and made unrepresentational and juxtaposed in strongly contrasting combinations. By the mid-1890s, most, if not all, of the Nabis produced book or magazine illustrations, or posters for the new theatres in Paris, such as the Théâtre de l'Oeuvre and the Théâtre des Pantins. Of the Nabis, Pierre

62 Bonnard was probably the most gifted poster designer. Inspired by Japanese woodcuts, his figures were depicted in silhouette and placed on the extreme edges of the composition. His 'France-Champagne' lithograph of 1894 provided a fine example of his *oeuvre* in this medium.

61 Henri de Toulouse-Lautrec drew on some of the techniques and imagery of the Nabis, with whom he had exhibited at Le Barc de Boutteville in 1892, and converted them into his own highly personalized graphic style. He produced a total of 32 posters, many for the popular entertainers and institutions of Montmartre: cabaret artists such as Aristide Bruant and Yvette Guilbert, and café-cabarets and music-halls such as the Moulin Rouge. Most of these are classics, showing his complete understanding of the basic function of the medium. His images are powerful and essentially two-dimensional, and easily read from a distance. Most importantly, they convey the specific persona of the client or product, portraying them where necessary in caricature. He used to the full the expressive quality of the line, transforming it as required into a nervous arabesque, or modulating it slightly to suggest an individual's character or gesture. Under his hand, the line became an almost independent carrier of the emotion.

60 The Swiss-born Théophile-Alexandre Steinlen was another successful graphic artist in Paris to respond to the new movement, although he never committed himself to it fully. His style was not explicitly in line with Art Nouveau until after his contemporaries, such as Toulouse-Lautrec, had shown their sympathies for it. His designs included posters and illustrations for newspapers and journals such as *La Chat Noire* and *Gil Blas Illustré*. He is today associated mostly with cats, which featured in many of his works.

63 Alphonse Mucha became the most celebrated Art Nouveau poster artist, in part through his association with Sarah Bernhardt, for whom he created several of his most memorable works. Born in southern

59 Gustav Klimt, *Judith and Holofernes*, oil on canvas, 1901

60 Théophile-Alexandre Steinlen, *Lait pur stérilisé*, poster, 1894

Moravia, a Slavic province of the Austro-Hungarian empire, Mucha moved in the mid-1890s to Paris, where he was put under contract by the lithographer Champenois. Champenois was quick to capitalize on Mucha's talent, transforming his designs into large editions of posters, menus, calendars and *panneaux décoratifs*, a more pretentious Belle Epoque type of poster.

Pushed by his entrepreneurial employer, Mucha produced a prodigious amount of work during the next five years. Individual posters and posters issued in series – such as The Seasons, The Precious Stones, The Arts, and The Times of Day – were anticipated with impatience by an insatiable public. In 1902, partly to meet this demand, Mucha published two volumes of his graphic designs, *Documents décoratifs* and *Figures décoratives*. These had the adverse effect of breeding numerous imitators, whose hackneyed copies helped to accelerate Mucha's fall from popularity towards 1910, around which time he returned to his homeland.

61 Henri de Toulouse-Lautrec, *Divan Japonais*, poster, 1892

62 Pierre Bonnard, *France-Champagne*, poster, 1894

63 Alphonse Mucha, *Monaco-Monte-Carlo*, poster, 1897

MONACO·MONTE·CARLO

AFFICHES ARTISTIQUES DE LA SOCIÉTÉ "LA PLUME"
31, Rue Bonaparte, PARIS.

Imp. F. CHAMPENOIS,
66, Boul! St. Michel, PARIS.

Mucha's characterization of the Belle Epoque maiden, with impossibly abundant hair radiating out in serpentine coils to fill the picture surface, was a romantic re-interpretation of Rossetti's *Proserpine*. Clad fashionably in jewelled or feathered headgear and immense sweeping skirts, this image of pure and naive youthfulness came to personify the mood in the French capital on the threshold of the new century. The image was employed with variable success by

67
68
other Parisian graphic artists, most notably Emmanuel Orazi and the versatile Georges de Feure. The latter, who had received his training under Chéret, designed posters for the Salon des Cent, Loïe Fuller and the Thermes Liégeois.

64
Eugène Grasset was another noted graphic artist in Paris to respond to the modern idiom, although with some hesitancy: his posters and book illustrations reveal clear English stylistic antecedents, particu-

65
larly those of Crane and the Pre-Raphaelites. Paul Berthon, Grasset's

94

pupil, likewise pursued a rather more formal and narrative style than that of Chéret or Mucha; many of his posters evoke a medieval charm and tranquillity.

In Brussels, van de Velde's versatility manifested itself in his designs for book illustrations, typography (for example, his series of initials published in *Van Nu en Straks* in 1893) and posters. Particularly notable was his 1899 design for the Tropon company, a food concentrate manufacturer, of a poster which consists of an arrangement of repeating abstract linear forms that rise from the bottom of the composition to meet a maze of rectangular lines that contain the single word 'Tropon' written in a formalized type face. The design's novelty lies in the fact that it is purely graphic; there are no pictorial elements whatsoever. 66

Far closer to the French interpretation of Art Nouveau were a host of Belgian poster designers headed by Privat Livemont, who had trained in Paris. Using the same iconography of nude, or semi-nude, Belle Epoque maidens who appeared so voluptuously on the billboards of Paris, Livemont placed them on backgrounds of stylized plants or on a bed of their own entwined tresses. The effect, which was always neat, fresh and colourful, proved popular among his clients, most of whom were commercial manufacturers. Henri Meunier, Adolphe Crespin and Fernand Toussaint generated a similar range of French *genre* posters, in which winsome young women promoted new household products or bicycles. 71

64 Eugène Grasset, *Avril*, page from a calendar, 1896

65 Paul Berthon, *Liane de Pougy*, poster for the Folies Bergère, *c.* 1900

66 Henry van de Velde, *Tropon*, poster, 1897

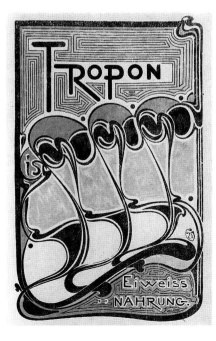

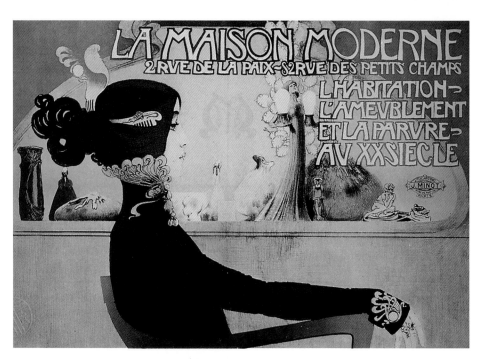

67 Emmanuel Orazi, *La Maison Moderne*, *c.* 1900–02

68 Georges de Feure, *Fashionable Lady*, oil on canvas, 1908–10

69 Peter Behrens,
The Kiss, poster, 1898

The Dutch painters Toorop and Thorn-Prikker included posters in their artistic repertory. Toorop's design of 1895, for Delftsche Slaolie, 70 is especially noteworthy in its transformation of long hair and plant organisms into complex linear patterns that animate the poster's entire surface. Thorn-Prikker's graphic style was also two-dimensional, but less decorative; his posters for the *Revue Bimestrielle pour l'Art Appliqué* (1896) and the Dutch Art Exhibition of 1903 reveal the tendency towards Expressionism that he pursued later in his career.

Posters in *Jugendstil* developed mainly in Munich, where Beardsley's influence is evident in the illustrative works of Markus Behmer and Thomas Theodor Heine, who together founded the satirical magazine, *Simplicissimus*. A far different decorative vernacular was adopted in the 1890s by Peter Behrens, who relied on simplified forms and single block colours to impart a modernist effect. His 1898 poster, *The Kiss*, provides a superior example of his ornamental style; the two 69 severe and almost classical profiles are enveloped in a dense arabesque of hair that draws them into, and finally unifies, the composition. Behrens's dedication page in 1900 for *Feste des Lebens und der Kunst* provides another interpretation of his organic style in its sinuous

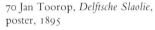

70 Jan Toorop, *Delftsche Slaolie*,
poster, 1895

71 Privat Livemont, *Cercle Artistique de Schaerbeek*,
poster, 1897

curvilinear geometric design. Otto Eckmann, Ludwig von Hoffmann and August Endell used a similar linear style derived from plant
forms.

The Vienna Secession, founded in 1897, formed its own avant-
garde publication, *Ver Sacrum*, to which progressive artists and
writers were invited to contribute. The magazine's format and
typography were characteristic of the new group in its crisp linear
quality and preference for a geometric matrix of ornamentation,
bearing clear witness to Mackintosh's influence. This architectural
quality of the Vienna School ensured its survival long after other
interpretations of the new art had become hackneyed, providing it
with a lasting foundation for modern design.

The influence of English artists on the Art Nouveau movement in
its entirety has already been described. In the field of graphics, the
forerunners were Blake, Mackmurdo, Beardsley and Crane. Charles
Ricketts and Charles Robinson contributed novel stylistic effects in
their illustrations for children's books and in their experimentation
with new type faces. In the field of poster art, the Beggarstaff Brothers

– William Nicholson and James Pryde – produced the best English examples in their woodcuts for the theatre (for example, *Don Quixote*), commercial products and magazines (especially *Harper's*). Their simplified shapes and bold colour contrasts reveal a strong Japanese influence.

In Glasgow, Margaret MacDonald applied the same stylizations to 72 her graphic work as she had to her earlier metalware and embroidery: elongated human forms and asymmetrical geometric patterns were rendered primarily in black and white. The introduction of one or two additional colours – such as pink for an isolated rose – softened the monochromatic impact of her compositions. From 1900, when she married Mackintosh, her work is often indistinguishable from his. Margaret's sister, Frances, worked in the same idiom in her designs for book covers and illustrations.

Likewise trained in Glasgow, Jessie M. King created illustrations for books printed by private presses, such as *Defence of Guinevere*, published by John Lane in 1904. Her graphic style, comprising spidery lines and intricate stippled detailing, was suitable for books and other small graphic work, such as ex libris plates, but not for posters.

72 Margaret MacDonald, *Queen of Diamonds*, from the *Four Queens* series, paint and gesso on wood, 1909

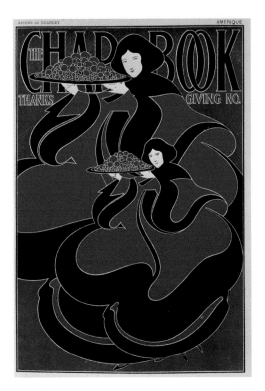

73 William Bradley, cover
for *The Chap Book*, 1894

73
In the United States, where European developments were readily
traceable in the art reviews of the era, William Bradley emerged as the
foremost draughtsman, illustrator and poster designer in the Art
Nouveau idiom. In addition to the artwork he produced for the
Chicago Tribune, *Echo* and *The Inland Printer*, Bradley published
several of his own magazines, including *Bradley: His Book*, which
contained examples of his own illustrative work and those of others
who showed modernist tendencies. Bradley's advertisement for
Whiting's Ledger Papers, depicting a Belle Epoque maiden seated
among poppies in a landscape within a broad foliate border, was
typical of work in 1900 and indistinguishable from the host of similar
images generated in France and Belgium at the time.

Louis John Rhead, who had emigrated to America in 1883,
designed bookbindings for the New York binder William Matthews
before turning his hand in 1894 to poster design. (Today, Rhead is
better known as a ceramist and china-painter.) Edward Penfield
likewise designed Art Nouveau-inspired posters, many for *Harper's*,
in a style reminiscent of Steinlen.

CHAPTER FIVE

Glass

The exhibition 'La Pierre, Le Bois, La Terre, et Le Verre', staged in Paris in 1884, provided unmistakable evidence that glass was undergoing an artistic revolution in France. Among the initiators were Eugène Michel, in Lunéville, and Eugène Rousseau, in Paris, 74 who separately explored new techniques and means of expression for the medium. Both experimented with cloudy, aerated and crackled internal effects, such as those found in moss agate, rock crystal and aventurine quartz. Metallic oxides were suspended within the glass, whose surface was deeply chiselled with relief images drawn from nature. Ernest Léveillé, Rousseau's pupil and then partner, continued 77 the search for this type of novel naturalistic effect.

Though such innovations were significant, they were quickly dwarfed by those of Emile Gallé, who from 1884 spearheaded the drive for change. A full review of Gallé's achievements in glass falls beyond the scope of this chapter, but his genius soon manifested itself in one after another work of breathtaking beauty and technical virtuosity. Early studies in horticulture were blended with his knowledge of literature, Symbolist poetry and a host of other influences that together provided him with an encyclopaedic glass-making repertoire. Early along the way, Gallé experimented with the enamelling techniques used by his father to decorate ceramic wares, and with Japanese and Islamic imagery, in which he followed the lead of Philippe-Joseph Brocard, who in the 1880s reproduced a range of Persian mosque lamps and vases in enamelled crystal.

Gallé was encouraged by the critics, who saw clearly the unrivalled importance of his essays in glass. Unlike his furniture designs, in which the congested imagery was seen to violate the nation's proud 18th-century cabinetmaking heritage, there were no deep-rooted traditions to be upheld in the field of glass. Among others, Roger Marx, the Inspector General of French Museums, was irrepressibly enthusiastic in his coverage of Gallé's displays at the annual Salons and world expositions. The public was likewise captivated; it soon

74 Eugène Rousseau,
imitation jade glass
jardinière, 1884–85

became *de rigueur* in fashionable circles to present one's tea-time host
with a bibelot by the Nancéien *maître verrier*.

Under Gallé's stewardship, glass became a protean art form. Until
then a static and colourless material to be painted or engraved with
pictorial images, it was now transformed into a medium of simulated
movement and infinitely blended colours, with complex internal
patterns and surface textures. Gallé's range of ornamentation, and its
manner of application to the vitreous mass, was even more
innovative. Techniques such as marquetry-de-verre, *intercalaire*
(inter-layered decoration), engraving, etching, patination, enamelling and the application or encrustation of pieces of glass, were mixed
ad infinitum in the pursuit of the perfect creation, most requiring an
additional trip to the furnace for the new decoration to be applied.
Further elements of his work, such as the poetic verses with which he
adorned many vessels (known for this reason as *verreries parlants*), and
his *verres hyalites* and *vases de tristesse* series, contributed to what had
become, by the time of his premature death from leukaemia in 1904,
the most comprehensive compendium of techniques in the history of
the medium.

Gallé's primary focus was nature, which provided him with an
inexhaustible source of creative inspiration. Flora of every species,
many indigenous to Alsace-Lorraine, were portrayed in their entirety
or in microcosm, such as the details of a calyx, pistil or corolla. He
found further artistic stimulus in a strange and creepy menagerie,

including the world of entomology – insects such as dragonflies, moths, beetles and ants – and the murky realm of the sea and its mysterious crustaceous denizens, which Jules Verne romanticized in *Twenty Leagues under the Sea*. 78

Gallé's overwhelming impact on the medium – both artistic and commercial – was quickly noted by other glasshouses, which began with varying success to generate a similar repertory of art glass. The most imposing of these was the neighbouring Daum works, which opened in Nancy in 1892. Mixing a range of techniques and images similar to that of Gallé, the Daum *frères* created several works of high aesthetic and technical quality amid a huge volume of commercial wares. The firm's light fixtures, mostly made in partnership with the 75 cabinetmaker Louis Majorelle, who manufactured their metal mounts, were especially distinctive and refined.

Beyond Nancy, inspired copyists included the Muller *frères* in 76 Lunéville and Croismare (Meurthe-et-Moselle), who in many of their

75 Daum *frères*, poppy lamp, glass with bronze foot, *c.* 1900

76 Muller *frères*, cameo table lamp, *c.* 1905–10

wares revealed a predilection for autumnal or twilight themes and hues achieved by their own etching technique, termed 'fluogravure'.

79 Also noteworthy were the creations of Burgun, Schverer & Company and Désiré Christian (the firm's chief designer and decorator between 1885 and 1903) in Meisenthal, a town in northern Alsace-Lorraine that had been annexed by Germany following the Franco-Prussian War of 1870. Remarkable iridized creations came from H.A. Copillet & Company, and its chief designer, Amédée de Caranza, in Noyon (Oise); engraved and etched glassware was produced by Legras & Company, in Saint-Denis (Seine), and by Vallerysthal & Portieux, in the Vosges region of north-eastern France. In Paris in the 1890s, the Pannier brothers designed several pieces of cameo art glass that were engraved for their firm, the Escalier de Cristal, by the Appert *frères*. In Belgium, the Cristallerie de Val Saint-Lambert in Seraing-sur-Meuse generated a similar, and often enchanting, selection of commercial art glass under the supervision of Louis Léon Ledru, a Parisian-born artist-designer.

Gallé's glass drew a host of other commercial imitators in France, both during his lifetime and well beyond. Some *genre Gallé* ateliers opened as late as 1930, only a year or so before the Gallé cristallerie itself closed. The imagery on these wares – flowers and wooded

77 Ernest Léveillé, crackleware goblet, *c.* 1889

78 Emile Gallé, *L'Herbier Maritime*, decorated glass vase, *c.* 1902

landscapes rendered *ad nauseam* in two or three layers of colour –
remained unchanged, irrespective of their date of creation. Among
80 many, the following bear mention: André Delatte, d'Argental, Arsall
and Richard, all in the north-east of France, in or near Lorraine;
Camille de Varreux (the art director of the Cristallerie de Pantin, who
used the pseudonym 'de Vez' in signing his wares), the Sèvres
manufactory, Louis Damon and Jules Mabut, all in Paris; and Jean
Noverdy, in Dijon.

The ancient technique of *pâte-de-verre* was revived towards the *fin
de siècle* by several French glass artisans, including Henri Cros,
François-Emile Décorchemont and Georges Despret, whose designs
were inspired by both traditional and modernist themes. In the latter
category was a range of studies drawn from nature – beetles, fish,
insects, etc. – modelled in high or bas-relief and rendered in a muted
palette. Younger *pâte-de-verre* artisans – those whose *oeuvre* reached
maturity slightly later, in the 1910s and '20s – retained the same
outdoor grammar of decorative ornament. Of special note in this
category were Gabriel Argy-Rousseau, of Meslay-le-Vidame; Jules-

79 Burgun Schverer & Company,
three marquetry vases, *c.* 1900–05

80 d'Argental, cameo glass and
wrought iron lamp, *c.* 1915–20

Paul Brateau, of Bourges; Albert-Louis Dammouse, of Sèvres; and
Henri Bergé and Amalric Walter, of Nancy.

The iridescent gold glassware of the Johann Loetz Witwe
glasshouse, located in Klöstermühle in western Bohemia, was of
sufficiently high quality and close resemblance to that of Tiffany for
the latter to initiate litigation in 1901 to prevent unsigned Loetz pieces
from being imported into North America. Under the artistic
direction of Max Ritter von Spaun, the Loetz firm generated a large
volume of industrial art glass that itself became the source of imitation
by regional competitors, including Pallme-König & Habel, in
Kosten; Wilhelm Kralik Sohn, in Eleonorenhain; and Gräflich
Harrachsche, in Neuwelt.

Loetz glassware consisted primarily of asymmetrical forms exe- 81
cuted in combinations of opaque colours enhanced with textured
finishes. The firm avoided in large part anecdotal or figural forms of
decoration, preferring to let the material's innate chromatic qualities
and plasticity dictate its appeal. In addition to the characteristic surface
iridescence of its gold pieces, a silvery-blue splashed, or drip, pattern

107

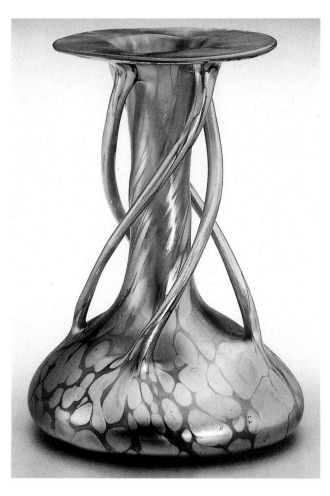

81 Johann Loetz Witwe,
vase with applied trails,
c. 1900

was applied to a brilliant cobalt or green ground with great
commercial success. Another decorative fillip involved the application to the body of the vessel of trailing handles or random prunts
that were given a gently crimped finish with the glassblower's
scissors. Some of the more ambitious pieces were applied in their final
operation with an openwork overlay of electroplated silver.

The modernist decorative vocabulary of most other Bohemian and
neighbouring Bavarian glasshouses in the 1900–10 years was bound
more to the area's rich heritage of traditionalism. Those firms that did
espouse the Art Nouveau idiom, such as Ludwig Moser & Sohn, in
Karlsbad, and Meyr's Neffe, in Adolf, did so hesitantly, with a broad

82 Louis Comfort
Tiffany, peacock
vase, c. 1893–96

nod to convention's forms and time-honoured decorating techniques, such as casing and engraving. A marked exception was the Glasfabrik Blumenbach of E. Zahn and M. E. Gopfert, in Blumenbach, which generated elongated flowerform vessels in clear glass applied with coloured flowers on trailing stems.

In Germany, the floral *Jugendstil* was epitomized in the glass confections of Karl Koepping, of the Glasfachschule Limenau. A chemist as well as a glass designer and blower, Koepping created a series of cups raised on tall undulating stalks evocative of old Venetian forms. Light and graceful, these were predictably fragile, and few, therefore, have survived. Friedrich Zitzmann, at some point Koepping's collaborator and then competitor, produced similar flower-form wares in Wiesbaden.

More Teutonic and traditional in form and inspiration was the production of the commercial glasshouse Petersdorfer Glashütte Fritz Heckert, in Petersdorf, for which Max Rude and Ludwig Sütterlin served as designers. Two other glass studios, those of Ferdinand von Poschinger, in Buchenau, and Maximilian Boudnik (address unknown), drew the inspiration for their iridescent and threaded organic wares from Loetz and Pallme-König.

In Scandinavia and Russia, word of the new movement came intermittently to glasshouses isolated both geographically and chronologically from developments in France and central Europe. The Kosta and Orrefors Glasbruks in Småland, southern Sweden, for example, introduced a range of cameo art glass in the Art Nouveau manner, but later than in the rest of Europe; in the case of Orrefors, where Simon Gate and Edward Hald led the search for a new idiom, this took place only around 1917. In St Petersburg, the Imperial Russian Court Glass Factory introduced a modest line of engraved modernist wares between 1905 and 1910.

Art glassmakers in England largely rebuffed Art Nouveau, as did their counterparts in other areas of the applied arts. In Stourbridge, the glass industry's hub, nature was interpreted warily at Thomas 83 Webb & Sons and at Stevens & Williams in a selection of conventionally formed cameo vessels engraved or etched with vignettes of stiff floral sprays frequented by butterflies and bees. The successors of John Northwood and George Woodall were more at ease in their depiction of mythological and other classical themes than with undue stylistic experimentation.

Across the Atlantic, the world of modern glass was dominated – if not monopolized, in the view of most critics – at the time by Louis 82 Comfort Tiffany. As with Gallé, the magnitude of Tiffany's achievements in the medium far exceeds a broad and general survey of Art Nouveau glass. Although his interpretation of nature varied significantly from that of his counterparts in the European Art Nouveau movement – he preferred to portray it realistically, in contrast to the stylistic abstractions that evolved on the Continent – Tiffany's preoccupation with the outdoors, and his general ideology on creation of art for the average household, placed him squarely within the new movement. Even so, he continued throughout his career to introduce traditionally inspired designs into the wares produced at his workshop in Corona, Long Island.

83 Thomas Webb & Sons, cameo glass vases, 1890s

More than anything else, it was Tiffany's manufacture of glass that set him apart from his contemporaries, most of whom had to depend on commercial glasshouses for their inventory. The establishment of the glass furnaces at Corona in 1893 effectively launched Tiffany on a new career of window-making, through which he could pursue the domestic American market directly. Until then he had worked largely for a single client, the church, in the creation of a wide range of liturgical items. Whereas many of these commissions (especially the memorial windows) had been arranged by individual members of a congregation, and therefore for the public at large, the church had

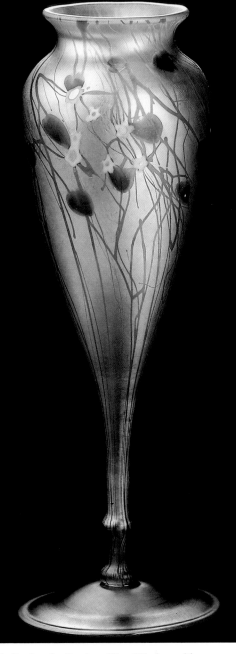

84 Frederick Carder, for Steuben Glass Works, gold vase, *c.* 1903

been Tiffany's principal client, and his primary means of access to other customers. The opening of the furnaces changed this, leading first to the production of a range of art glass, and then to various other art forms offered to the public through both the firm's showroom and a network of retail outlets across the country.

By his own account, Tiffany's search for a new variety of glass took him thirty years, at the end of which he could boast, 'I have found means to avoid the use of paints, etching, or burning, or otherwise treating the surface of the glass . . . I can make any shade of glass in pot metal.' Examination of a selection of his glass (which he patented under the name 'Favrile') reveals that he grossly understated his achievements in this field. By mixing up to seven colours, thrown together from different ladles, his staff could produce a giddy range of blended hues, many mottled or deeply veined to simulate nature's ever-changing moods and palette. The sheets obtained were often treated with an iridescent surface finish created in a heating chamber, where an atomized solution of metallic vapours was sprayed onto the final piece. The process gave a kaleidoscopic lustre to the glass, which became a principal characteristic of the firm's domestic wares.

Whereas most of Tiffany's designs – for windows, lamps and vases – were, as noted, realistically portrayed, the firm's output did include some delightful Art Nouveau stylizations, particularly in hand-blown art glass pieces. Foremost among these was a series of floriform vessels in which the plant's roots, stem and petals were fashioned into a single attenuated organism.

The Steuben Glass Works of Corning, N.Y., were second only to Tiffany in the United States in the creation of modern art glass. Incorporated to manufacture the crystal and coloured glass blanks that were decoratively cut by Thomas G. Hawkes & Company, and named after the county in which it was located, Steuben in 1903 prevailed on the Englishman, Frederick Carder, to leave his employment as art director at Stevens & Williams, the famous Stourbridge glasshouse. Under Carder's stewardship, Steuben introduced a wide range of techniques and artistic effects into its repertoire over the next three decades. Whereas some of these, such as the gold-and-blue Aurene series and Diatreta vessels, bore in their forms, colouration and surface lustre a close resemblance to existing Tiffany Favrile models, others were clearly innovative (in the United States, at least). Notable among them were the firm's editions of Verre de Soie, Tyrian, Ivrene, Intarsia, acid cut-back and *cire-perdue* wares. Other techniques introduced during Carder's tenure (for example,

84

Cluthra and Cintra) took their inspiration from 19th-century developments at English glasshouses, such as Christopher Dresser's designs for James Couper & Sons.

Philip Julius Handel provided a different aesthetic from Tiffany's in a range of modern lamp designs produced at his glassworks in Meriden, Conn. He may have created certain Tiffany-style leaded glass floral shades, such as the wisteria and apple blossom models, but Handel established for himself a measure of individuality in a series of mould-blown and lightly etched glass shades adorned with hand-painted studies of flowers, landscapes, or exotic birds, mostly rendered in an autumnal palette. Other Handel glass household appliances, likewise made of decorated blown glass, included humidors, night lights, tazzas and demi-tasse cups and saucers.

Several other American glasshouses manufactured floral glass lamps after 1900 with varying commercial success. Duffner & Kimberly in Manhattan created a range of Tiffany-style leaded shades. In New Bedford, Mass., the Pairpoint Corporation was responsible for one innovation – a series of blown shades, entitled 'Puffies', that were moulded in high relief with the contours of the flower represented on the shade. Bigelow & Kennard of Boston were also active in this field.

Like Gallé, Tiffany drew a host of imitators, not only when his glassware was at the height of its popularity around 1900, but also well into the 1920s. Among the first of these was the Quezal Art Glass & Decorating Company, in Brooklyn, which was formed in 1901 by two ex-Tiffany employees, Martin Bach and Thomas Johnson. Bach had been a batch mixer at the Corona glassworks and therefore knew the secret ingredients and formulae of Tiffany's Favrile wares, while Johnson had been employed there as a glassblower. The two, who were joined shortly by two more ex-Tiffany artisans, the glass decorator Percy Britton and the gatherer William Wiedebine, produced a shameless range of Tiffanyesque household wares, including vases and lampshades. Distinctive among these was a range of flowerform vessels with broad undulating mouths, similar in form to Tiffany's jack-in-the-pulpit models, which in their brightly lustred surfaces and crisp green and gold pulled feather decoration, rivalled the beauty of Tiffany's prototypes.

The firm, which had taken its name from the quetzal, a Central American bird with brilliantly coloured plumage, remained in operation until 1925, during which time it failed to introduce into its repertoire any noteworthy shapes or techniques.

85

85 Pairpoint
Corporation, 'Puffy'
Apple Tree lamp,
c. 1910

The Vineland Flint Glass Works was another firm to specialize in Tiffany-style domestic glasswares. It was established in Vineland, N.J., around 1900 by Victor Durand, a descendant of the Baccarat family in France, who had emigrated in 1884 to the United States, where he joined the itinerant labour force that serviced the nation's glasshouses. Durand used a range of decorative motifs similar to those of both Tiffany and Quezal – heart-shaped leaves on entwined trailing stems, bands of striated peacock feathers, a quilted pattern which the firm termed 'King Tut', etc. – but he did introduce some novelties, including a deeply crackled surface finish (created by immersing the finished piece in cold water before it was fully annealed) that resembled the fissures in volcanic rock, and, as a finishing technique applied to the surface of some vase and lampshade models, a membrane of threads that was appropriately named 'Spider Webbing'.

Three Ohio houses produced glassware that was often undistinguishable from that of Quezal and Durand: the Fostoria Glass Specialty Company, established in 1899 in Fostoria; the Imperial Glass

Company in Bellaire; and the Fenton Art Glass Company in Martin's Ferry.

The stock-in-trade of several American glasshouses established after World War I shows how difficult it was for the industry to rid itself of Tiffany's monolithic influence, even so long after Art Nouveau had fallen out of fashion and Tiffany's creations themselves had become bland and perfunctory. By the 1920s, Tiffany was no longer actively involved in the Corona production, which led to his decision in 1928 to sell the glasshouse to A. Douglas Nash, the son of Tiffany's first plant manager, Arthur J. Nash. For a brief period Nash continued the production of gold lustred tablewares, to which he added a range of Chintz, Diamond Optic, and Aventurine models.

A mid-European version of Art Nouveau ornamentation was pursued in the Unites States at the turn of the century by two glassmakers: the Honesdale Decorating Company, set up as an art glass subsidiary in 1901 in Honesdale, PA, by C. Dorflinger & Sons; and Carl V. Helmschmied, an ex-Bohemian resident of Meriden, Conn. Both eschewed Tiffany's iridescence and organic forms for items of traditional shape decorated by traditional techniques. Vases made of cased, or 'flashed', glass – ruby or topaz over a clear layer, for example – were engraved or painted with flowers and Belle Epoque maidens evocative of the glassware of the Mont Joye glasshouse in France and the Teplitz ceramic manufactory in Bohemia.

Other American glassware sometimes grouped under the Art Nouveau umbrella includes the production of three houses located in the East: the Mount Washington Glass Company in New Bedford, Mass., the New England Glass Company in Cambridge, Mass., and Hobbs, Brockunier & Company in Wheeling, West Virginia. All three manufactured a selection of shaded peach-amber-ruby coloured art glass that was broadly termed Peachblow or Amberina. Today, these wares appear distinctly Victorian in style, rather than Art Nouveau, in their use of Louis XV- or Louis XVI-style metal mounts and generous applications of frilled or pinched glass bands. Still other glasshouses around 1900 offered an uninspired mix of traditionalism and modernism; they included the Libbey Glass Company in Toledo, Ohio, the Phoenix Glass Company in Monaca, PA, and the Boston & Sandwich Glass Company in East Sandwich, Mass. But none of these could be looked on as a meaningful contribution to Art Nouveau.

CHAPTER SIX

Ceramics

Towards the turn of the century, ceramics underwent a far quieter revolution than most of the other disciplines in the decorative arts. This may have been caused in part by the absence of the individual genius and assiduous self-promotion of a Lalique in jewelry, or a Gallé and Tiffany in glass. Another consideration is the fact that ceramics lacks the spontaneous impact of gems that sparkle or glass that radiates colour and light. By the nature of its components and its opacity, the medium is a rather contemplative or mood-evoking one, relying more on the viewer's connoisseurship of such complex issues as clays and glazes, and their often unpredictable fusion by fire, than on dramatic visual effects. It is, in short, a medium of the heart rather than the eye.

The ceramists of the Art Nouveau movement – ranging from individual potters and small *ateliers* to large commercial manufactories – can be grouped broadly into three technical categories: those who specialized in glazes, sculpting (or modelling) and painted forms of decoration. On many occasions, of course, two or all three of these techniques were used by craftsmen in concert.

As in the case of glass, it was in France that the first movement for change in the world of ceramics took place. Théodore Deck is generally credited with extricating the medium from the clutches of historicism from around 1860. Deck rejected conventional china painting techniques of decoration in favour of ancient Persian, Turkish and Far Eastern pottery, in which the glaze itself, rather than a pictorial or narrative type of imagery, was pre-eminent. Among his developments in the field of glazes, Deck developed the distinctive blue-green turquoise glaze that still bears his name today.

It should be noted that for Deck, and for most of the French ceramic community, the Japanese influence was pervasive in the late 1800s: independent potters sought to rediscover the glaze and stoneware formulae of Japan, while the commercial factories drew eagerly on the iconography of its blue-and-white porcelains.

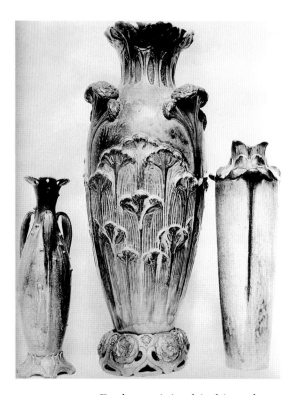

86 Emile Decoeur, three stoneware vases, *c.* 1902

Deck was joined in his early experimentation by Félix Bracquemond, the engraver and lithographer, and then later by several ceramists who came to maturity at the *fin de siècle* – in particular, Edmond Lachenal, who founded his own studio in Châtillon-sous-Bagneux, where he invented a process of gilding on faience. Lachenal was typical of the many individual French potters who experimented at the time with glazes and stoneware; among them were Emile Decoeur, a student of Lachenal, whose *oeuvre* was characterized by delicate blue, pearl grey, celadon and ivory glazes, and Etienne Moreau-Nélaton, who developed a style of ornamentation consisting of *champs* (fields) filled with monochromatic glazes. Another noted member of the Deck school was Henri Simmen, who applied his stoneware with fiery *sang-de-boeuf* (ox-blood) and *peau de lièvre* (rabbit's skin) glazes. Simmen was the consummate potter in an Arts and Crafts context, handling every stage of the manufacturing process himself: the creation of the glaze, the mixing and throwing of the clay, and its decoration and firing. His approach, which was based on trial-and-error rather than scientific formulation, was typical of those

86

individual potters around 1900 who rebelled against the encroachment of mass production on their craft.

Unlike Simmen, most ceramists maintained a standard division of labour, in which the pots were thrown or moulded by one artisan and decorated by another. For the Art Nouveau glaze exponent, the only importance of the clay body was that it provided the surface to which he could apply his glaze formulae. Symmetrical forms, many of classical or Oriental inspiration and lacking relief decoration, were therefore commonplace. The standard household vase became the perfect vehicle, since it could serve as a functional container while masquerading as a work of art.

To the modernist glaze exponent around 1900, personal artistic expression was achieved through a perfect blend of ingredients, which, when fired at the predetermined temperature, provided the surface texture, opacity and colour sought. The vagaries of the kiln could be counted on to provide some happily unforeseen results. Over-firing, for example, which burned away the glaze, could lead to imperfections such as unevenness of colour, veining, blistering or splotching. These, however, often added felicitous nuances of tone and individuality to the completed piece.

A prominent ceramist among the many masters of Art Nouveau glazes was Pierre-Adrien Dalpayrat, who was raised in Limoges, from   87

87 Pierre-Adrien Dalpayrat, stoneware vase with a *rouge flambé* glaze, c. 1897

where he pursued his career in Bordeaux, Toulouse, Monte-Carlo and again in Limoges, before settling at the age of 45 in Bourg-la-Reine. Assisted by his wife and three sons, and in association sometimes with Ernest Chaplet, Dalpayrat was drawn to sumptuous high-fired Chinese glazes, particularly those of the Ming and Ch'ing dynasties. His special interest lay in a range of thick liver-red *rouge flambé* glazes imitative of *sang-de-boeuf*, which became his signature colour, and a range of marbleized and crystalline glazes that he poured in two-colour combinations to create dramatic chromatic effects. Dalpayrat worked with faience, porcelain and, especially, stoneware, to which he sometimes applied elaborate ormolu mounts.

One of modernism's earliest proponents, Ernest Chaplet, in 1875 joined the ceramic *atelier* at 116 rue Michel-Ange, in Auteuil, in the 16th arrondissement of Paris. Established by Charles Haviland, the son of the American David Haviland who had founded a porcelain workshop in Limoges in 1842, the Auteuil *atelier* was intended for experimentation, but soon developed an independent line of faience

88 Ernest Chaplet, stoneware
pitcher, *c.* 1898

89 Auguste Delaherche, ceramic plate, *c.* 1903   90 Clément Massier, plate, 1892

and stoneware. Chaplet worked to develop a range of Japanese-
inspired pottery which concentrated on the interplay of translucent
glazes and the simplification of pictorial elements. From 1882, at his
own studio, named L'Art du Feu, on the rue Blomet in Paris-
Vaugirard, Chaplet created a range of *sang-de-boeuf*, jaspered and
marbleized glazes which he applied to sober forms. His work was
praised by the critics.

    Auguste Delaherche was another *fin-de-siècle* ceramist of diverse
talents. Trained initially as a painter and glassmaker, and then in
silversmithing at Christofle, he concentrated from 1887 on ceramics.
He was instructed at the Auteuil workshop by Chaplet, whose studio
he purchased. Delaherche quickly developed a distinct range of high-
fired *flambé* and mat glazes, which he soon supplemented with others
of variegated or two-toned colouring. From 1894, at his new studio in
La-Chapelle-aux-Pots, he added to his earthenware production a
range of glazed porcelain pieces engraved or reticulated by the *ajouré*
technique in imittation of Chinese rice-grain porcelain.

    In 1872, a ceramic enterprise was founded in Golfe-Juan by
Clément Massier. The workshop's early designs, inspired by Hispano-Moresque and Renaissance prototypes, were phased out
gradually as Massier explored metallic lustrewares, with the assistance
of the painter Lucien Lévy-Dhurmer. Combinations of iridized glazes
– green-violet, red-purple, mauve-orange and a shimmering blue –

88

89

90

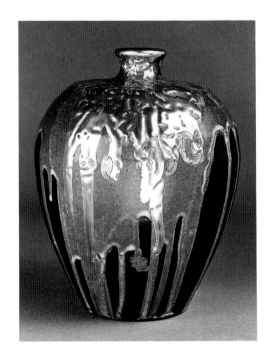

91 Jean Carriès, stoneware
vase, 1892

92 Georges Hoentschel,
ceramic vase, 1898

93 Paul Jeanneney, ceramic
covered jar, c. 1902

were fired at extremely high temperatures, often over diffused images
of maidens and flowers. Massier's distinctive and kaleidoscopic
lustreware drew several imitators, particularly the Zsolnay manufactory in Pecs, Hungary, and Samuel A. Weller, of Zanesville, Ohio,
who named his pottery's lustreware 'Sicardo' in recognition of the
Frenchman, Jacques Sicard, a former assistant of Massier's, whom
Weller hired around 1901.

91   Jean Carriès was one of the first to challenge the inertia within the
French ceramic industry, following the 1878 Exposition Universelle.
Embracing ancient Japanese stoneware techniques, Carriès, who died
in 1894, created a wide range of three-dimensional works – grotesque
masks, portraits, fruit, newts, goblins, vegetables and toads – executed
sometimes in blue-and-brown glazes tinged with green, and in high-
fire combinations that generated oxidized metallic surface patterns.
Of his many students, Alexandre Bigot and Georges Hoentschel
emerged around 1900 as successful exponents of Art Nouveau.

    Bigot was trained as a chemist and developed an interest in Oriental
ceramics following the 1889 Exposition Universelle. He established
his *atelier* in his native village, Mer (Loire-et-Cher), where he
practised between 1889 and 1900. His pottery production, mostly in a

characteristic blend of chestnut-brown, turquoise, copper-red and lemon-yellow glazes, consisted in part of architectural and sculptural commissions in glazed faience – plaques, friezes, chimney surrounds and monuments – for Guimard's Castel Béranger, and for Bourdelle and Jouve, among others. Hoentschel, a decorator-ceramist by profession, was another *fin-de-siècle* craftsman drawn to the Art 92 Nouveau idiom, which he interpreted with flamboyance in various media, such as furniture and *boiserie* for the pavilion of the Union des Arts Décoratifs at the 1900 Exposition Universelle, and a range of Japanese-inspired ceramics, some with ornate organic bronze mounts.

A third Carriès disciple, Paul Jeanneney, generated a limited 93 production of asymmetrical vessels in restful, if not sober, hues enhanced on occasion with crystalline encrustations.

As a kind of footnote to the history of the medium, it should be noted that Paul Gauguin experimented in clay and terracotta between 1886 and 1893 as a means of exploring the interrelationship between plastic materials and colour. He is believed to have created roughly seventy works, many of which evoke an Art Nouveau imagery in their subject-matter, symbolism and tonality.

94 Taxile Doat, two *plaques* and three vases, 1902

Like Bigot, Emile Muller produced a range of architectural stoneware, termed *grès Muller* as a result of its wide use, at his small manufactory in Ivry, near the French capital. Part of his output of murals, garden statuary and ornaments was in the Art Nouveau mode, for sculptors and artist-designers such as Frémiet, Chalon, Constantin Meunier, Fix-Masseau, Grasset and Alexandre Charpentier.

Taxile Doat, who was born in Albi, studied design and ceramics at the Ecole Adrien Dubouche in Limoges and the Ecole des Beaux-Arts in Paris. Soon famous for his mastery of the *pâte-sur-pâte* technique that he developed with Marc-Louis Solon at the National Manufactory of Sèvres, Doat was by 1900 a legendary figure within his field. His skills were prolific, including the production of a heterogeneous range of *flambé*, crystalline, crackled and metallic glazes, which he shared with the industry in his book *Grand Feu Ceramics*, published in

1905. His designs were as varied as his glazes, and included fruit- and vegetable-formed vessels such as the colocynth (bitter apple) and gourds, plus masks, plaques, bottles, dishes, paperweights and portrait medallions. On some pieces he left areas of the ceramic body unglazed to create a novel aesthetic effect. 94

Doat was invited in 1909 by Edward J. Lewis, a local entrepreneur and art lover, to advise the American Women's League in University City, Missouri, on the construction of its new art pottery. Later that year, he accepted the directorship of the University City Pottery, where he collaborated with some of America's foremost artist-potters, including Robineau, Rhead and Dahlquist. He returned to France in 1915.

André Metthey, based in Asnières, was one of the first Art Nouveau ceramists to be inspired by Carriès, although he chose to invite a host of noted painters and sculptors, among them Bonnard, Denis, Derain, Maillol, Matisse and Redon, to decorate much of his *oeuvre*. In this manner, Metthey could concentrate on the development of new glazes and moulding and stamping techniques, in all of which he showed a rich talent. His *flambé* glazes were especially successful. 95

In Nancy, ceramists adopted the naturalistic imagery applied by Gallé and his School to all their creations. Most of Gallé's own essays 96

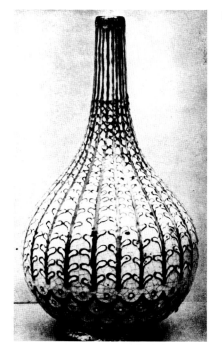

95 André Metthey, ceramic vase, 1903

96 Emile Gallé, ceramic vase,
1880s

in the medium were undertaken early in his career, in his father's
ceramic workshop in Saint-Clermont. His decorative vernacular was
inspired at the time particularly by *Japonisme*, and many of his faience
pieces reflect this in their depiction of fans, seals and blossoms on a
gold ground. Towards 1900, several other local potters, particularly
Ernest Bussière and the Mougin *frères*, Joseph and Pierre, used the
medium with more vigour and success. The Nancéien *pâte-de-verre*
glassmaker, Amalric Walter, also tried his hand on occasion at
decorating pottery pieces.

Many other individual French ceramists were drawn to the Art
Nouveau movement at the height of its fashionableness. Some, such
as Emile Lenoble, Paul Beyer and René Buthaud, used the experience
as a stepping stone to celebrated careers that reached their peak in the
inter-war years. Others, such as the Swiss-born Edouard Sandoz, who
designed *animalier* studies in porcelain for Haviland and Sèvres,
achieved final recognition in other disciplines. Others again, such as
Raoul Lachenal (Edmond's son), and Henry-Léon-Charles Robhal-
ben, produced several modernist works of high artistic and technical
merit.

97

Many potters introduced three-dimensional effects on to their
wares by modelling the clay while it was still damp and pliable.

During the Art Nouveau era much of this relief ornamentation was organic in theme – bands of buds and stalks that protruded from the surface of the vessel, but were integrated into it by the subsequent application of the glaze. Carved, or incised, detailing sharpened the definition.

In contrast to the Art Nouveau studio potter, France's large commercial manufactories – for example, Sèvres, Limoges and Vincennes – preferred the Victorian painterly form of decoration to that of the glaze, which was subject to the accidental effects of the kiln and therefore too random for mass production.

A seemingly infinite iconography of images – mostly those of the floral sprays and flower-bedecked maidens that dominated the other minor arts of the Belle Epoque – were painted onto clay or porcelain bodies by artist-decorators, often with a strong Japanese interpretation. The Barbotine technique, which incorporated the application of translucent liquid underglaze clay slips developed by Haviland, was

97 Raoul Lachenal, six vases, 1904

especially popular, as was *impasto*, adapted from painting to ceramics in 1872 by Chaplet, among others. In *impasto*, blended gradations of colour, applied freely and thickly and in deep and brilliant hues, provided startlingly life-like effects.

Founded in the 18th century and overhauled in 1891, the National Manufactory at Sèvres mixed tradition and modernism in 1900 within a large repertory of glazed and painted forms of decoration. Among its most gifted Art Nouveau practitioners were Albert Dammouse, Marc-Louis Solon and Edouard Cazaux, who came to prominence in the 1920s. The firm's *fin-de-siècle* production included editions of bisque and porcelain figurines and household appurtenances by noted sculptors and artist-decorators, such as Agathon Léonard, Raoul Larche and Georges de Feure.

Beyond France, the Art Nouveau movement in ceramics took on both national and regional characteristics, but with obvious cross-fertilization between centres. Its interpretation in northern Germany and Scandinavia, where it was adopted for serial production around 1900 by the large manufactories, was especially successful. In

98 Royal Danish Porcelain Factory, ceramics, *c.* 1905

100

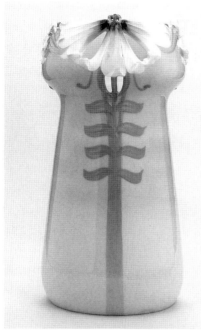

99 Nils Erik Lundstrom, for Rörstrand, porcelain vase, c. 1900

100 Albert Dammouse, ceramic vase, 1903

Copenhagen, at the Royal Danish Porcelain Factory, under the artistic guidance of Emil Krog, and at Bing & Groendahl, a graceful anthology of flowers, insects, crabs and algae were rendered in a soft palette of powder-blues, pinks, greens, and greys, on a white ground. These underglaze images were often executed in shallow relief, a modelling technique which brought realism and refinement. A similar painterly repertory of radiant flowers was generated from 1896 at Rörstrand, outside Stockholm, by the artist-designer Alf Wallander.

98

99

In Berlin, the tradition-bound Königliche Porzellan-Manufaktur (K.P.M.) embraced *Jugendstil* tentatively after the arrival of Theodor Schmuz-Baudiss in 1902, with a selection of curvilinear and floral patterns on some of its tableware services and vases. The Staatliche Porzellan-Manufaktur at Meissen did the same by retaining outside designers, including van de Velde and Behrens, to provide it with state-of-the-art modernism. The firm's 'Wing' pattern of 1901–02, by Konrad and Rudolf Hentschel, was warmly received by the public

129

101 Rosenthal Porcelain Company, porcelain cup and saucer, *c.* 1902

and critics alike. Further south, the Nymphenburger Porzellan-Manufaktur, in Bavaria, produced a similar line of *Jugendstil* tablewares under the supervision of the artist-engraver Hermann Gradl, while at Villeroy & Boch, in the Saar, a less pronounced interpretation of modernism was marketed under the firm's brand name, Mettlach. Two other German manufactories, Rosenthal in Selb, and Swaine & Co. in Hüttensteinach, approached the new movement with hesitancy.

Few independent potters in Germany appear to have involved themselves with Art Nouveau. A noted exception was Max Läuger, a mixed-media artist-craftsman, who produced a range of *Jugendstil*-inspired vessels at his studio in Kandern in the Black Forest.

The Low Countries provided Art Nouveau with a vivid palette, particularly at the Rozenburg works, near The Hague, where the chemist M.N. Engelden introduced in 1899 a wafer-thin 'eggshell' porcelain which was used to create a delightful line of Art Nouveau-inspired wares decorated by J. Kok, J. Schellinck and W.P. Hartgring, among others, in a style evocative more of Java in the Dutch East Indies than of Japan. Among the other Dutch potteries that produced Art Nouveau wares, mention should be made of Haga, in Purmerend, owned by Wed.-N. Brantjes, which closely imitated Rozenburg's ornamentation; Amphora in Oostgeelt-les-Leiden, where the designer Christian Johannes van der Hoef oversaw a line of modernist designs between 1894 and 1910. The Amstelhoek factory, in Amsterdam and Gouda, likewise flirted briefly with Art Nouveau.

In central Europe – in Austria-Hungary and what is now the Czech and Slovak states – Art Nouveau ceramic production was generally far more commercial than to its north. With the marked exception of certain Viennese workshops – those of the Wiener Keramik and the Vereinigte Wiener und Gmundnerkeramik, both of which had access to Wiener Werkstätte artist-designers such as Josef Hoffmann, Berthold Löffler, Dagobert Peche, Michael Powolny and Otto Prutscher – design was geared to popular taste. In Teplitz, at Amphora (unrelated to the one in the Netherlands) and at Royal Dux, 102 a large volume of ceramic vessels and sculpture, the latter imitative of the languid bronze *femmes-fleurs* at the Paris Salons, was produced. Many wares were encrusted with coloured glass cabochons and accented in gold. A comparable range of faience pieces was offered by Ernst Wahliss in Vienna. At Pecs (Hungary), Vilmos Zsol and his son Miklos generated a range of brightly-coloured lustreware at the family firm of Zsolnay.

The Italian manufactories of L'Arte della Ceramica and Figli di G. Cantagalli in Florence, and that of Richard in Turin, drew on the same forms and grammar of ornament as the Danish factories. Slender vases enhanced with formalized flower sprays rendered in fresh colours provided a far more elegant product than those in nearby Bohemia.

In Britain, the late Victorian ceramic community was pre-occupied more with an eclectic range of revival styles, including Gothicism, *Japonisme*, Islam and their own Aesthetic Movement, than with European Art Nouveau. Certain attempts were made, however, to expore the new modernism, although mostly in a somewhat debased and commercial manner.

William Moorcroft, who in 1897 assumed the directorship of art 103 pottery production at James MacIntyre & Co., in Burslem, designed a range of 'Florian' wares that were decorated with formalized arrangements of flowers and peacock feathers applied by an

underglaze transfer-printing process in which the images were outlined in trailing slip. Some of the firm's other painted wares, such as the 'Pomegranate', 'Hazeldene', and 'Claremont' series, reveal the same restrained English awareness of avant-garde Continental design. At Doulton & Co., in Lambeth, London, a different interpretation of Art Nouveau was achieved in the pictorial landscapes by Florence and Hannah Barlow, and Eliza Simmance. Minton's in Stoke-on-Trent, Staffordshire, provided a version of the European modernist movement in its 'Secessionist' wares designed by Louis Solon and John Wadsworth.

By far the most intriguing and comical designs of the epoch were those of the four Martin brothers, Walter, Robert-Wallace, Edwin and Charles. Operating as a family business, situated first in Fulham

105

102 Amphora, pair of earthenware vases, c. 1900

103 William Moorcroft, 'Florian' ware vases, 1899 (left) and 1900 (right)

and then in Middlesex, the four generated a wide range of salt-glazed stoneware, of which a bestiary of mythological beasts and grimacing grotesque birds became the most celebrated.

Specific attention to glaze development was paid by Bernard Moore, who moved from Longton to Stoke-on-Trent in 1906. Moore pursued a very personal figurative style, mostly in a range of copper-red glazes fired at both low and high temperatures onto stoneware or porcelain. The Ruskin Pottery, founded by William Howson Taylor in 1898 near Birmingham, likewise experimented with glazes, especially *flambé*, lustred and crystalline varieties fired at high temperatures on Chinese-inspired vessels.

Across the Atlantic, the ceramic industry at the turn of the century was divided roughly along the lines of its European counterpart;

104 George Ohr, ceramic vase, c. 1900–06

105 Martin Brothers, pair of salt-glazed stoneware face jugs, 1892

individual potters and studios explored recent glaze and modelling innovations, while the larger manufactories opted for a painterly, and commercially more viable, decorative vernacular. Either way, there were some startling innovations.

Among the glaze exponents, several craftsmen achieved masterly and unorthodox results. Hugh C. Robertson, for example, pursued dramatic visual and textural effects at the Dedham Pottery with a rich mix of multi-coloured glazes and drippings that created volcanic and bubbled surface textures when fired at very high temperatures. Even more eccentric, both in temperament and artistry, was George Ohr, the 'mad potter' of Biloxi, Mississippi. Ohr manipulated his thin clay vessels with a variety of finishing techniques, including crimping, ruffling, pleating and crushing.

Others, such as Theophilus A. Brouwer, Jr., at the Brouwer Pottery, and Cornelius Brauckman at the Grand Feu Art Pottery, pursued a more restrained and conformist style of personal expression. Frederick H. Rhead at the Roseville Pottery Co., and Arthur E.

104

106

134

106 Frederick H. Rhead,
earthenware pitcher or vase,
c. 1900

107 Ruth Erikson, for the Grueby
Pottery, ceramic vase, 1905

Baggs at the Marblehead Pottery, explored modern glaze formulae,
as did larger studios such as the Chelsea Keramic Art Works, the
Merrimac Pottery Co., the Pewabic Pottery and the Waller Pottery.

107   Well known internationally at the time was the Grueby Pottery, of
Boston, which had exhibited, to favourable reviews, alongside the
Tiffany Studios stand at the 1900 Exposition Universelle. The appeal
of the firm's mat green glaze lay both in the rich monotone of its
colouring and in its velvety, yet glossless, surface – qualities
considered unique at the time to American pottery. Until then, dull
finishes had been obtained either by sandblasting or by the immersion
of the piece in an acid-bath. The patterning on some Grueby pieces,
where the uneven application of the glaze resulted in paler green
veining, led to the coinage 'cucumber' or 'watermelon rind' to

136

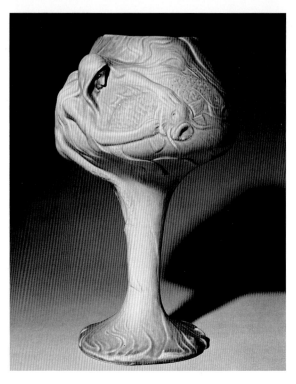

108 Artus van Briggle, *The Toast* Cup, ceramic chalice, 1901

109 Fulper Pottery, ceramic vase with a copper-dust crystalline glaze, 1918–22

describe the firm's wares. Like Grueby, the Roseville Pottery of Zanesville, Ohio, concentrated on its line of glazes, which were carved on occasion to provide additional ornamentation.

At Tiffany Studios, experimentation in monochromatic glazes began sometime before 1906, when Tiffany announced his entry into the pottery field. Boldly sculpted pieces, moulded in full relief as vegetables or flowers, were glazed in complementary earth tones of ivory, beige, brown, green or ochre. The Gates Potteries, for whom its president, William Day Gates, designed a range of architectonic wares marketed under the brand name 'Teco', similarly concentrated on single glazes, especially a mat green variety that was used on some Art Nouveau-inspired floral vases.

The Fulper Pottery of Flemington, N.J., developed a range of glazes inspired by Chinese *famille-rose* ceramics, which had eluded ceramists since their discontinuation two centuries earlier. It displayed these on vessels modelled appropriately as Oriental beakers, temple jars and globular bottles. The individual potter Artus van Briggle, who had moved from the Rookwood Pottery in Ohio to Colorado

110 Tiffany
Studios, lotus
bowl, Favrile
pottery, *c.* 1905

111 Fritz Albert,
for the Gates
Potteries, 'Teco'
ceramic vase,
1904–05

112 Rookwood
Pottery, ceramic
vase, decorated
by Kataro
Shirayamadani,
1899

Springs in 1899, was also drawn to the mat glazes of ancient China, which he applied to his wares, some of which were adorned with Art Nouveau figures sculpted in high relief.

The Rookwood Pottery in Cincinnati was by far the most important in the field of painted ceramics, generating a prodigious amount of high-quality wares for five decades, from its inception in 1880. Its stable of artist-decorators included many of exceptional skill, such as the Japanese-born Kataro Shirayamadani and Matthew Andrew Daly, both of whom rendered themes from nature in a delicate Art Nouveau palette. The Newcomb College Pottery, in New Orleans, likewise embellished its wares with depictions of the outdoors, many of them provided with incised detailing to outline the separate components of the design.

It is appropriate to close with a brief reference to Adelaide Alsop Robineau, to many observers the most complete potter of the age. Conservative by nature, Robineau did, however, make stylistic concessions to Art Nouveau in a few of her creations. The perfection of her craftsmanship – in particular, her mastery of a wide range of techniques, including the laborious one of excising – and her development of a range of mat, glossy and crystalline glazes, drew the attention and respect of the international ceramic community.

112

CHAPTER SEVEN

Jewelry and Fashion

French jewelry at the turn of the century can be divided stylistically into two broad categories: *joaillerie* and *bijouterie*. The search for a form of nomenclature to provide a clear distinction between the two preoccupied the jewelry industry in the late 19th century, in part because of the interrelationship between them and a third discipline, that of the *orfèvrier*, or worker in precious metals. Henri Vever, in his three-volume *La Bijouterie Française aux XIX Siècle*, was one of several contemporary jewelers to attempt a convincing classification; but the debate has never been resolved. For the purposes of this book, *joaillerie* applies to those jewelers who were governed by the intrinsic value of the materials they employed; those whom I shall include under *bijouterie* felt, conversely, that artistic interpretation was a more important criterion in the determination of the true worth of a piece of jewelry. Though both groups sought to be modern, they achieved this through different means of artistic expression and with a preference for different materials.

Joaillerie represented the mainstream of traditional French jewelry. Its strict preference was for precious stones and metals over less expensive alternatives. Gem-set jewelry, then as now, had an inherent value – measured by the carat-weight of the stones – which, in turn, determined to a considerable extent its value in the marketplace. Carats were the jeweler's currency. Clearly, therefore, the *joaillerie* industry in mid- and late-19th-century France depended, as elsewhere at the time, on an elite and moneyed clientele composed mainly of aristocrats, landed patrician families and the small but growing band of *nouveau riche* bourgeoisie who were reaping the financial rewards of the Industrial Revolution. Most of the populace could not afford real jewelry, and for them manufacturers of costume jewelry provided a range of imitations in glass and other inexpensive coloured materials, such as garnets and cameos.

In the 1860s, the French jewelry industry was mired down in historic revivalism – imitations of Etruscan, Henri II, Charlemagne,

Renaissance and Louis XIII prototypes enjoyed brief bouts of public popularity – and the critics railed against the lack of artistic integrity and innovation within the *métier*. Rejuvenation was discernible first in the 1870s, particularly in the designs of Oscar Massin, the eminent Second Empire jeweler, whose compositions were later determined to have anticipated the Art Nouveau movement. Massin introduced a modest degree of naturalism and fluidity into his floral compositions, although today his changes seem often hesitant, or barely perceptible. A further indicator of the change to come was provided at the 1889 Exposition Universelle by Lucien Falize's display of gold bracelets adorned with pansies, violets and carnations.

Towards 1900, the *joaillerie* industry remained anchored in traditionalism. It responded to the Paris Salons' emerging infatuation with nature by creating a range of gem-set jewelry that, in its rationalization of naturalist forms, acknowledged the new aesthetic. Its proponents, including major jewelry houses such as Boucheron, Falize, Vever, Sandoz, Coulon & Cie. and Félix Desprès, intended a quiet revolution that would ensure the retention of its traditional hierarchy of precious materials while bowing to modern artistic impulses. Throughout this transition the diamond ruled supreme; its

116
113,115

144

113 Henri Vever, jewelry, Paris Exposition Universelle 1900

114 René Lalique, pendant, enamelled gold, chalcedony and baroque pearl, *c.* 1898–99

incorporation in all major commissions, such as those for European royalty, remained a prerequisite. If not the focus of the piece of jewelry, it was used in clusters of large stones or in glittering fields of *pavé*-set smaller ones that served to accentuate the central composition. Introduced in this manner, often interspersed with coloured gems, the diamond's fiery inner beauty allowed it to survive the charges of exclusivity aimed at it by Art Nouveau jewelers. Part of its appeal lay in the irreproachable manner of its presentation: each setting represented a celebration of the lapidarist's art.

The 1900 *joaillier*'s preferred motifs, often drawn from the Louis XVI period, included garlands of acanthus or oak sprigs, arabesques, dentils and festoons. Other classical styles – including a *mélange* of

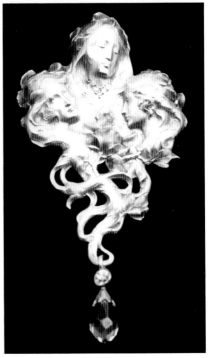

115 Falize *frères*, gold and enamel lily brooch set with diamonds, *c.* 1897

116 Boucheron and Edmond Becker, *Les Trois Filles d'Eve*, brooch, 1897

mythological, hieratic, Assyrian, Byzantine, medieval, Renaissance and Oriental – provided fabulous winged dragons, bacchants, chimeras, scarabs, gorgons and a host of similar images from art history's lexicon. Insects, such as butterflies and beetles, were interpreted in the same formal, and therefore largely stiff and lifeless, manner.

Bijouterie was the style of choice for most of the new generation of jewelers who were drawn from the mid-1890s to the Art Nouveau movement. Many of them lacked the funds necessary to buy expensive gems, so they were naturally receptive to the alternative concept that stressed design. Soon an entirely new range of stones – some semi-precious, but others merely colourful – was introduced into the jewelry shown at the Salons, including chalcedony, chrysophase, zircons, amethysts, opals, topazes, jades and agates. These provided a palette of inexpensive stones that could simulate the more pricey ones. Nor did the revolution stop there, largely because of Lalique's experimentation with other unconventional materials, such as horn and tortoiseshell, both of which could be carved and patinated. Ivory was another surface used widely by *fin-de-siècle* jewelers to provide sculpted detailing.

Equally important to the new movement was the revival of the Renaissance art of enamelling, which enjoyed huge popularity around 1900 in the capable hands of Eugène Feuillâtre, André Fernand Thesmar, Georges Fouquet and, of course, Lalique. Not only were enamels used to replicate the colours of precious gems, but they could be shaded to provide striking realistic effects in portraits, or to impart feelings of depth, limpidity and luminescence. Further variation was achieved through the use of three enamelling techniques mastered by contemporary Japanese enamellers: those of *plique-à-jour*, *champlevé*, and *cloisonné*.

The substitution of these modestly priced materials for those conventionally used made the price of *bijouterie* significantly lower than that of *joaillerie*. This, in turn, attracted to the medium a broader and less affluent clientele. Likewise, many art connoisseurs, previously denied access to the jewelry market because of its expensiveness, now began to frequent the Salons in search of affordable items.

The 1900 Exposition Universelle confirmed the pre-eminence of the French jewelry industry. Predictably, pride of place was reserved for René Lalique, who had first drawn the attention of the critics at the 1895 Salon of the Société des Artistes Français with his display of seventeen pieces of jewelry and sketches of four others in preparation. His choice of radical naturalistic designs and of materials unassociated with the jewelry trade drew spirited reviews and the first inkling for many that a *bona fide* modern movement was under way. Lalique's display two years later, at the Brussels Exposition, secured his position in the vanguard of the 'new art', but it was only in 1900 that the French public at large could see and begin to comprehend the magnitude of his genius.

It is not possible in this book to give more than a brief acknowledgment of the stupefying originality, penetrating beauty and technical virtuosity of Lalique's jewelry. Many books have been 114,118 written on the master *bijoutier* and *verrier*; his was the unique jewelry talent of his age, comparable only to that of Benvenuto Cellini during the Renaissance. It is sufficient here to note that he was the true initiator of the French Art Nouveau movement in jewelry and, from the start, its dominant force. It was Lalique who first rebelled against

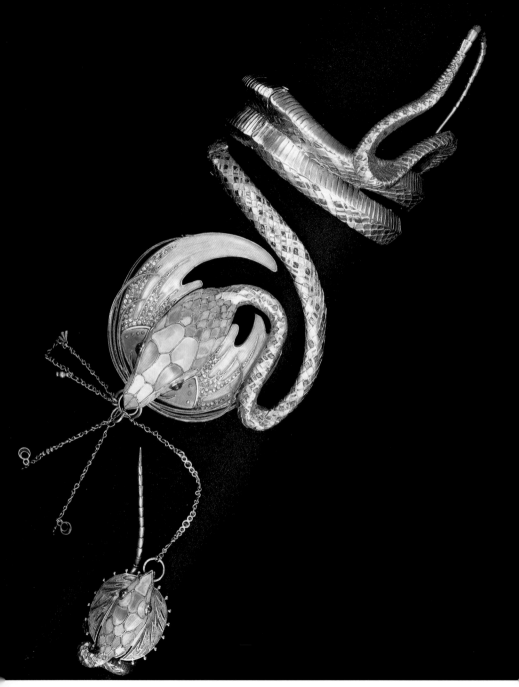

117 Georges Fouquet, gold serpent bracelet, set with a mosaic of opals, enamels, rubies and diamonds, made for Sarah Bernhardt, 1899

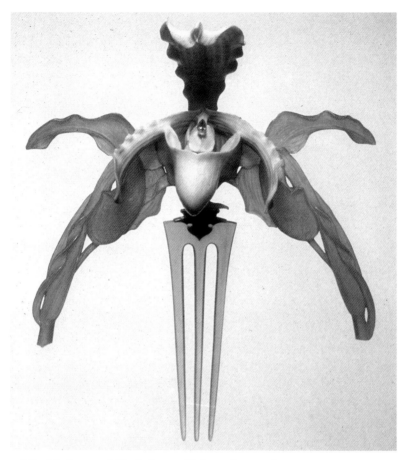

118 René Lalique, *orchidée* diadem, gold, ivory, horn and topaz, *c.* 1903

the tyranny of the diamond, until then the stock-in-trade of the jeweler's art.

Predictably, Lalique's vast celebrity generated a host of imitators, only a few of whose creations showed the same high level of artistry: most notably Georges Fouquet, Lucien Gaillard, Charles Boutet de Monvel and Henri Vever. To varying degrees, all these craftsmen drew on the same imagery, although that of Boutet de Monvel often spilled over into a range of nightmarish themes that today seem

117,119
113
121

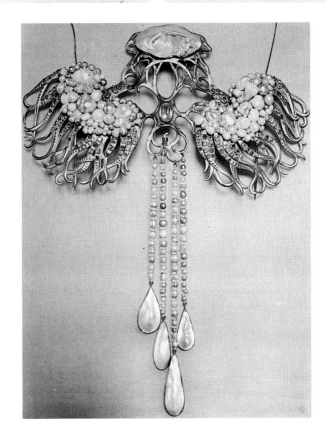

119 Lucien Gaillard, gold pendant with diamonds and *plique-à-jour* enamel *c.* 1902

120 Lucien Gautrait and Léon Gariod, gold and enamel pendant set with diamonds, topazes and emeralds, *c.* 1900

121 Charles Boutet de Monvel, pendant, 1903

122 Edouard Colonna, gold and green enamel pendant with pearl drop, *c.* 1898

totally unsuitable for items of personal adornment. Nothing is known of another prominent *genre Lalique* jeweler, Lucien Gautrait, beyond the fact that his designs were executed by the Parisian jeweler Léon Gariod. 120

An entirely different modernist interpetation was adopted among the top designers retained by Bing's Maison Art Nouveau and La Maison Moderne of Meier-Graefe: Edouard Colonna, Georges de Feure, Maurice Dufrène, Paul Follot and Emmanuel Orazi. Here the inspiration was clearly the abstract convolutions and arabesques of van de Velde and his Belgian cohorts. 122

The 1900 *bijoutier* drew on the same range of motifs as did his counterparts in other disciplines, particularly the producers of small household accessories and *bibelots*. Most of these motifs were rampantly Art Nouveau, including studies of the outdoors and depictions of draped and sensual young women. Sometimes Woman and Nature were merged into a hybrid *femme-fleur* or *femme-libellule*. Modern interpretations of history's *femmes fatales*, such as Salome or Leda, likewise made their appearance on every type of jewelry, as did real-life celebrities such as the entertainers Loïe Fuller and Cléo de Mérode, who were similarly transformed into a range of idealized female adornments.

151

123 Alphonse Mucha
and Georges Fouquet,
bodice ornament,
enamelled gold,
emeralds, baroque pearl
and watercolour on
mother-of-pearl, *c.* 1900

Nature was treated marginally better. The French countryside, in
particular, provided a wellspring of inspiration for the nation's
jewelers. Common garden species such as forget-me-nots, irises,
marguerites, thistles, satinpods, mistletoes and wisteria were rendered
with great sensitivity both as entire plants and in detailed studies of
their individual components, such as pistils and corollas. Even humble
domestic cereals – wheat and barley, for instance – were elevated
briefly to an exalted artistic plane.

The formal distinction between *joaillerie* and *bijouterie* was
frequently blurred in the attempt by their adherents to find a middle

ground that would appeal to both constituencies. The large traditional jewelry houses, especially, sought to accommodate both styles in their pursuit of a modernist vernacular. Further stylistic dilution occurred as artist–designers from other fields were drawn to jewelry, particularly *bijouterie*. Various hybrid jewelry styles evolved, each with its own characteristics. Prominent among these were the *bijoux de peintres*, in which the central element of the jewelry was painted, on ivory or some other flat surface, and set within a surround of precious materials. The graphic artist Alphonse Mucha completed   123
a series of pieces for Fouquet in this manner that included miniature portrait medallions depicting languid maidens. Mucha's creations were boldly new and theatrical, but not jewelry *per se*: most pieces were over-sized and impractical to be worn except on stage by his most celebrated client, Sarah Bernhardt.

Another *bijouterie* variant was medal-jewelry (described at the time as both *broche-medaille* and *medaille-bijou*), which was made of bronze or gold brooches cast, often in bas relief, with Art Nouveau subjects such as nymphs and night creatures. Among its exponents were Jules Desbois, Edmond Becker, Victor Prouvé and Charles Rivaud. Today   116
these pieces seem quaint souvenirs rather than serious essays in contemporary jewelry design.

Beneath the aura and mystique of the Belle Epoque lay some harsh truths: the majority of the population was underprivileged, under-paid and underfed. Life for the French working classes was a treadmill devoid of such fashion niceties as new jewelry and visits to the couturiers in the Faubourg Saint-Germain. *Le tout Paris* consisted only of that small part of the capital that 'mattered', i.e., the titled and moneyed upper classes captured for posterity on canvas by the society painters Giovanni Boldini, Georges Clairin and Jacques-Emile Blanche. It was this exclusive *haut monde*, whose social calendar included the opera, Maxim's, Longchamps racecourse and carriage rides in the Bois de Boulogne, for whose favours the jewelers of the day vied. Even allowing for the set's assorted circle of hangers–on, including actresses, courtesans and demi-mondaines, the actual number of those who determined the fashion standards of the day was minute, well below 50,000. Yet their every move and romantic intrigue, charted in popular periodicals such as *L'Illustration*, *Vanity Fair* and *The Tatler*, mesmerized the rest of the populace.

Parisian jewelers took their lead at the turn of the century from the city's premier couturiers, such as Charles Frederick Worth, Redfern and Jacques Doucet, and then, from around 1910, Paul Poiret. Each new change in fashion made it necessary for jewelers to review their existing inventory: for example, plunging necklines exposed the neck and shoulders to the possibility of a new line of chokers and pendants. Sleeveless dresses bared the arm, likewise providing the opportunity for a new selection of bracelets and arm-bands. Muffs, however, concealed the hand, wrist and lower arm, thereby reducing the demand for bracelets and rings. Victorian bustles supplied ample surfaces of silk and tulle for the display of jewelry types such as corsage ornaments, parures and pectorals; yet when Poiret later eliminated whalebone corsets from his fashion repertoire, such visibly heavy pieces became *démodé*. The new order transformed the female silhouette. Suddenly, dresses were long, tubular and relatively unadorned, which led, in turn, to the need for a smaller scale and more understated line of jewelry and accessories.

Changing hairstyles and hat fashions also affected jewelry forms and functions. Long hair and bonnets required pins to secure them, but long hair could conceal the ears, and thus, earrings. On the other hand, shortly coiffed hair, such as the chignon or, slightly later, the *garçonne* or bobcut, revealed the ears and upper neck. Bouffant hair styles invited the use of diadems, tiaras, and elaborate combs and hair ornaments.

Traditional *joaillerie* survived the Belle Epoque, regaining much of its earlier glory after World War I in the gem-studded Art Deco creations of Boucheron, Cartier, Chaumet and Van Cleef & Arpels. To its adversaries at the turn of the century, however, it remained a status symbol rather than a vehicle for good design: a diamond's size and sparkle were not enough to assure that a piece of jewelry was a work of art; artistry was required, too.

Predictably, the glut of Art Nouveau jewelry that flooded the Paris Salons between 1900 and 1905 led quickly to the movement's collapse and, as a result, that of the *bijoutier*. Lalique's sublime creations were parodied in countless vulgar and servile imitations, which led to disillusionment among the devotees of Art Nouveau. Those who had never particularly liked the new art, but had felt compelled to embrace it due to its high fashionability during the Belle Epoque, made an even more rapid retreat.

Beyond France, most European modernist jewelers took their early lead from that of the Parisian avant-garde. German *Jugendstil* jewelry, for example, at first showed a propensity for floral ornament (in the late 1890s) before a more distinctly national, and abstract and linear, style evolved (1900–10). Notable in the former category were Robert

124 Wilhelm Lucas von Cranach, brooch in gold, enamel with a baroque pearl, diamonds, rubies, amethysts and a topaz, 1900

Koch in Baden-Baden, Karl Rothmüller in Munich, and the artist Wilhelm Lucas von Cranach, all of whom created high-style images of flower-bedecked maidens with long trailing tresses. Later, though, most jewelers adopted a more conservative stylistic approach to the new art; in Berlin, for example, classical forms were merged with attenuated plant motifs which showed a greater affinity for Brussels than for Paris. 124

Pforzheim, a city bordering on the Black Forest, became the thriving centre of the German jewelry industry around 1900. Most workshops offered a wide range of commercial wares, many for the foreign market, in which *Jugendstil* represented only one of numerous styles represented. A large volume of local production was in poor taste and made of inferior materials, such as low grade silver or Britannia metal adorned with enamels. In Pforzheim, the firms of Theodor Fahrner and F. Zerrenner were noteworthy for their production of inexpensive high-style Art Nouveau jewelry. In Hanau, another large German jewelry centre, traditional diamond-set jewels predominated over the new movement and its less costly materials.

A more austere Vienna Secessionist style of ornamentation was pursued by the jewelers in the artist's colony in Darmstadt, including

Patriz Huber, Peter Behrens, Ludwig Habich and Hans Christiansen. Olbrich's rare designs for brooches and pendants evoke the stark verticality and decoration of his architecture.

In Vienna, the jewelry created by the Wiener Werkstätte replicated the designs of its household accessories, such as toiletry boxes and handmirrors. Neat geometric contours housed crisp arrangements of cubes, spirals, coils, volutes and heart-shaped leaves in the manner of the English Arts and Crafts movement. Preferred materials were silver and silver-gilt set with cabochons of semi-precious stones or mother-of-pearl.

Austrian production of jewelry in the modern idiom was meagre. Pride of place was reserved for the designs of Josef Hoffmann and Koloman Moser; Moser's were often more stylized. Among others who designed jewelry for the Wiener Werkstätte were Berthold Löffler, Otto Prutscher, Karl Witzmann and Eduard Wimmer. Less distinctive were the related designs of the students and staff at the Kunstgewerbeschule.

Only two Austrian jewelry workshops appear to have adopted the ideals of French Art Nouveau: A.D. Hauptmann and Roset und Fischmeister. Gustav Gurschner transformed miniaturized versions of his high-style figurative sculpture into a few articles of personal adornment.

There was just one jeweler and *orfèvrier* in Europe who could attempt to measure up to Lalique – the Belgian, Philippe Wolfers. Wolfers created a breathtaking array of jewelry and precious *objets d'art* at the turn of the century in the context of French Art Nouveau, many of which he exhibited at the Paris Salons, perhaps as a direct challenge to the master French *bijoutier*. Mixing enamelled gold and silver with precious and semi-precious stones and ivory with great facility, Wolfers drew on many of the new movement's most shocking and extravagant themes for his artistic repertoire, such as sinister night creatures and the mythological Medusa. His style retained its own unmistakable identity and originality, despite its clear French influence, but was passed over by other Belgian artist-designers in preference for that of van de Velde.

Van de Velde used his deceptively simple and smoothly flowing line, often looped or turning back on itself, to produce an elegant range of jewelry rendered in silver or gold set with amethysts and emeralds.

Among his followers in Brussels were the jewelers Paul Dubois and Leopold van Strydonck, who was a member of Les Vingt.

156

125 Josef Hoffmann, silver gilt necklace set with citrines, made by the Wiener Werkstätte, *c.* 1904

126 Philippe Wolfers,
La Nuit, pendant, 1899

127 Luis Masriera, gold
jewelry, 1900–05

Scandinavian jewelers at the turn of the century remained largely unaffected by the new movement. A noted exception was Georg Jensen, in Copenhagen, who interpreted it with a streamlined, almost serene and lyrical simplicity of form and imagery. Jensen's rounded jewelry forms, often enhanced with cabochons of amber, moonstones and other inexpensive coloured gems, echo those of his hollow- and flatware silver production.

Also in Copenhagen, and a source of great influence on Jensen in his formative years, were the metalworkers Mogens Ballin and Thorvald Bindesboll, who included a similar range of modern jewelry in their repertory.

Far to the south, in Barcelona, Spain's only Art Nouveau foothold, the jeweler Luis Masriera was another to fall under Lalique's spell. On **127** returning from the 1900 Exposition Universelle, Masriera abruptly ceased the production of traditional jewelry at his family workshop and introduced a modern range *à la Lalique*. He managed to retain a distinctive personal style, however, in which his images of *fin-de-siècle* and medieval maidens and flowers were depicted in full or high relief on a gold ground inset with *plique-à-jour* enamelled panels and tiny brilliants. A charming aspect of Masriera's jewelry (mostly pendants

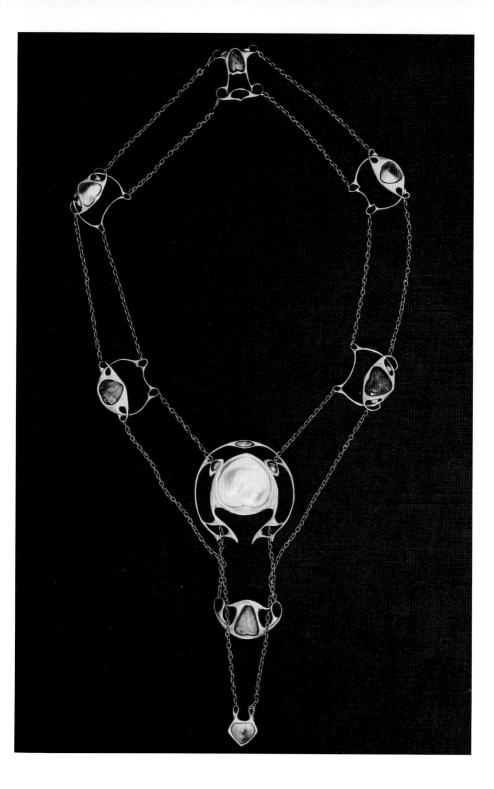

and brooches) was his use of articulated elements, as in the joints of dragonfly wings, that allowed them to tremble realistically when the wearer moved.

In England, Liberty & Company's production of jewelry was 128 synonymous with much of the nation's interpretation of the modern art. Interlaced or knotted Celtic-revival motifs – the same range as that adopted by the firm for its Cymric and Tudric silver and pewterwares – appeared in jewelry enriched further with shaded peacock enamelled panels and cabochons of semi-precious gems, such as turquoise. Designs by Archibald Knox were interchanged with those of Oliver Baker, Bernard Cuzner and Rex Silver. Jessie M. King, a noted Glaswegian book designer and graphic artist, also created jewelry designs for Liberty in her characteristically spidery style. Executed by W.H. Haseler & Son of Birmingham, Liberty jewelry was offered in silver and gold.

Several individual English jewelers and jewelry designers were similarly drawn into the pursuit of a novel style to combat the tradition-oriented dreariness of late Victorian design. Most of them, however – for example, C.R. Ashbee, Arthur and Georgie Gaskin, 129 Ella Naper and Frederick James Partridge – were closer in spirit to the

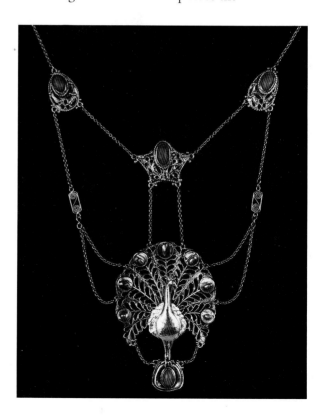

128 Archibald Knox and W.H. Haseler & Son for Liberty & Company, gold *entrelac* and mother-of-pearl necklace, *c.* 1902

129 C.R. Ashbee, peacock necklace in silver, gold, coral and black mother-of-pearl, *c.* 1900

130 Unger Brothers and William B. Kerr,
mass-produced silver brooch, *c.* 1900

Arts and Crafts movement than to the Art Nouveau of the Continent. Greater emphasis was placed on the handcraftsmanship of their wares (and on the accompanying social ideology), than on an association with a faddish, and certainly suspect, international decorative arts movement. In many instances the distinction is barely discernible: both movements sought a simple and symmetrical refinement in opposition to historicism. Mass-produced Art Nouveau jewelry in England appears to have been the domain of only one manufacturer: Charles Horner, of Halifax.

Taking its lead from Europe and England, the jewelry trade in the United States embraced the new movement around 1900, as it had *Japonisme* and the Egyptian revival a decade or two earlier. The two principal commercial centres for jewelry manufacture, Providence, R.I., and Newark, N.J., therefore generated a range of inexpensive Art Nouveau items – brooches, buckles, pendants, sash clasps, lorgnettes, combs and hat pins – for America's new fashion-conscious middle and merchant classes. Belle Epoque maidens, rendered in profile framed by the luxuriant coils of their hair, were die-stamped in low-grade silver for the mass market. As in the related field of silver 130 production for the popular taste, the firms of Unger Brothers and William B. Kerr were predominant in this aspect of jewelry manufacture. Another large silver manufacturer, the Gorham Corporation of Providence, created modernist jewelry in silver, silver-gilt and copper in a vigorous style that seemed to draw inspiration from current craft revival philosophies.

A higher quality of design and materials was achieved by Marcus & Company in New York, and Peacock & Company in Chicago. Both

131 Louis Comfort Tiffany, necklace with grape and vine motifs,
gold, enamel, and opals, *c.* 1904

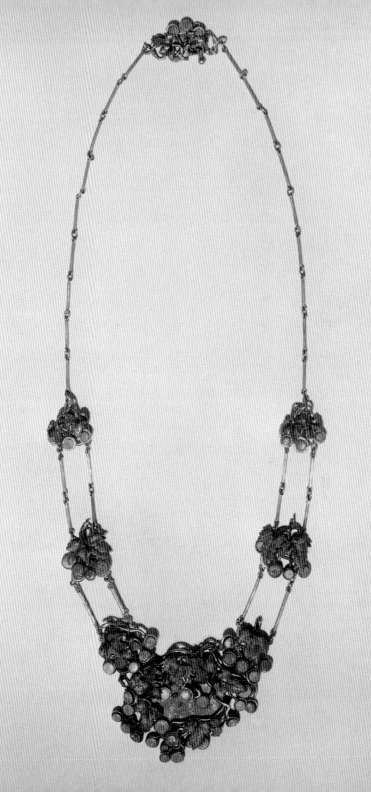

offered a range of French-inspired Art Nouveau floral jewels remarkable for their liberal use of bright enamels.

131   Louis Comfort Tiffany's foray into the world of art jewelry began before the death of his father in 1902, and his subsequent appointment as Art Director of Tiffany & Company, a position he held in conjunction with the management of his own decorative arts firm, Tiffany Studios. This formal link with the family's jewelry firm provided him with increased access to, and familiarity with, its jewelry operations. Characteristically, however, Tiffany conducted his initial experiments in jewelry design in private, and the extent of the cooperation between him and Tiffany & Company has remained uncertain.

Tiffany retained Julia Sherman to oversee his jewelry production, at first requiring her to use her name when ordering supplies in order to conceal his involvement. A small studio was established on 23rd Street in Manhattan, where Sherman and her staff translated Tiffany's jewelry cartoons into finished works. Early pieces were hand-wrought in a distinctly robust, if not rudimentary, style, far removed in spirit from the traditional wares manufactured at Tiffany & Company. An even greater distinction between the two was Tiffany's choice of inexpensive stones and enamels in preference to the large gems and lavish settings that were the hallmark of Tiffany & Company's creations. Tiffany preferred modestly priced Mexican opals, tourmalines, pearls, demantoids and carnelians. As in the case of Lalique, the value of his jewelry lay in its artistry and colour harmonies, not in the intrinsic worth of its gemstones. Tiffany's favourite jewelry themes were organic: dandelions, wild carrot, grape clusters, bittersweet, blackberries and Queen Anne's Lace.

CHAPTER EIGHT

Silver, Metalware and Objets d'art

Silver manufacturers at the turn of the century opted for the known over the unknown. Reprints of old pattern books were scoured for enduring styles and models in preference to a search for a new decorative idiom. Orthodoxy prevailed, even in an industry over-hauled by modern technological advances.

Paris attracted most of the era's most famous silversmiths and *orfèvriers*, several of whom – René Lalique and the Houses of 134 Boucheron, Aucoc and Linzeler, for example – were better known in 133 the related field of jewelry. The four annual Paris Salons served as the barometer by which the French silver industry could monitor both its own progress and that of its individual members. Work after work of extraordinary artistry was presented at the Salons between 1900 and 1905. Quite simply, the scope and scale of the *objets d'art* created by both individual craftsmen and the larger houses at the time repudiate the more vulgar essays in the name of the new art in other disciplines.

In its resistance to change, the French silver industry adopted Art Nouveau imagery tentatively. Most members of La Société Pari-sienne d'Orfèvrerie and established firms like Cardheilac, Aucoc, Christofle, Boucheron and Keller chose to offer a limited selection of Art Nouveau-inspired silver and objects of vertu within a broad repertory of styles. They were generally more adventuresome, though, in their introduction of novel materials into their new creations, a practice for which Lalique had crusaded for many years. Precious and semi-precious metals and stones were mixed with base, and often unconventional, materials such as enamel, mother-of-pearl, horn, tortoise-shell and lacquer.

Lalique's awesome presence in the world of decorative arts extended to a range of luxury household accessories – *épergnes*, mirrors, utility boxes, etc. – created with the same inimitable refinement and technical virtuosity that characterized all his work. His principal interest around 1900, however, was jewelry, and his achievements are therefore described earlier in this book.

137   Lucien Gaillard was another Art Nouveau artist-designer to apply himself as both *bijoutier* and *orfèvrier*. Drawing strongly on entomological and zoological themes, Gaillard transformed nature's humblest, and sometimes ugliest, creatures – rhinoceros beetles and praying mantis among a multitude of bugs, snakes and other reptiles – into a graceful selection of vases, humidors and other domestic utensils, many in the Japanese taste. Part of Gaillard's brilliance lay in his mastery of a wide range of metals, woods, horn and patinations,

136   which he blended effortlessly. Henri Husson, from Alsace, was another craftsman to show great versatility, producing the bulk of his Art Nouveau works for the Paris foundry- and gallery-owner Adrien A. Hébrard.

Also in Hébrard's stable of designers was Carlo Bugatti, the eccentric Italian who moved to Paris in 1904 after closing his cabinetmaking shop in Milan. During his sojourn in the French capital, Bugatti produced for Hébrard silver and *vermeil* wares populated with a bizarre menagerie of creatures: fantastical elephants,

142   wart-hogs, ostriches and crocodiles, over all of which hovered a ubiquitous dragonfly.

Other artist-craftsmen at the Salons adorned their *objets d'art* with enamel executed by the three traditional processes: *cloisonné, plique-à-jour* or *champlevé*. The best-known exponents were Eugène Feuillâtre,

132   the father-and-son team of Fernand and Emile Thesmar, and Etienne Tourrette, who inserted *paillons* (spangles) into the enamel to

132 Fernand Thesmar, cups, gold with *plique-à-jour* enamel, *c.* 1900

133 Lucien Hirtz, for Boucheron, silver water pitcher, *c.* 1900

134 René Lalique, chalice with ivory and silver, 1901–03

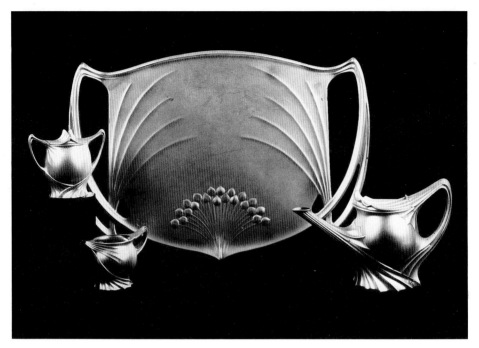

135 Paul Follot, silver-plated metal tea service, *c.* 1902

heighten its reflection potential. Invariably of a highly intricate and precious quality, Art Nouveau enamelwares included small bowls, compotes and toiletry boxes.

There were many more metalworkers of distinction at the Salons between 1900 and 1910, among them Jules Habert-Dys, Lucien Hirtz (who worked for the House of Boucheron), Georges Bastard, Lucien Bonvallet and Valéry Bizouard, who came to maturity after World War I as silver designer for Maison Tétard.

The Swiss-born Jean Dunand was another metalworker who made his debut at the Paris Salons in the early years of the 20th century. Later celebrated as the era's foremost Art Deco *ferronnier* (metalworker), Dunand worked first in *dinanderie*, the art of encrusting precious metals (gold and silver) upon base ones (copper and brass). The craft is referred to also as damascening after the ancient technique perfected in Damascus.

168

136 Henri Husson, tray, bronze with copper encrustations, *c.* 1908
137 Lucien Gaillard, rhinoceros beetle vase, bronze with wood base, *c.* 1905

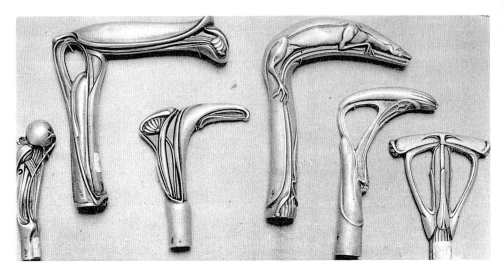

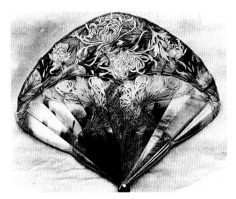

138 Georges de Feure, walking stick handles, silver, *c.* 1902

139 Adolphe Truffier, wall sconce, gilt-bronze with malachite, amethysts and emeralds, 1901

140 Georges Bastard, fan, carved horn with encrustations of gold and mother-of-pearl, 1906

141 Jules Habert-Dys, silver caviar server with inlaid enamel, 1905

In the United Kingdom, silvermaking was one of the few crafts at the turn of the century to embrace the Art Nouveau idiom. It did so reluctantly, however, largely avoiding the exuberant floral and abstract curvilinear interpretations prevalent on the Continent. Enamels and semi-precious stones were chosen as the best means of expressing a modernist impulse, along with delightful Celtic Revival imagery. Most silver production, however – both in form and in design – either remained traditional or showed other late Victorian influences, such as those of the Aesthetic Movement, *Japonisme* or the rigorously handcrafted style of the Arts and Crafts guilds.

143 Liberty & Company dominated the production of English Art Nouveau metalware. Its lines of silver and pewter, introduced under the trade names Cymric (pronounced Koomric) and Tudric respectively, were a huge and immediate commercial success. Apparently confident of their continuing appeal, the firm also offered in its Regent Street store a selection of wares by its European competitors, including Orion Zinn, J.P. Kayser & Sons, Orivit and Walter Scherf & Co.

Liberty produced a wide range of Cymric and Tudric domestic wares around 1900, ranging from standard items such as porringers, christening sets, biscuit barrels, muffin dishes, egg coddlers, and hollow- and flat-ware, to costly gifts such as sporting trophies and punch bowls. The most ambitious of these were accented in bright

142 Carlo Bugatti, silver and ivory tea service, *c.* 1910

143 Archibald Knox for Liberty & Company, vase, enamelled silver with turquoise *cabochons*, 1904

144 Archibald Knox, Tudric pewter mount with green glass bowl made by James Powell & Sons, 1904–06

enamels and/or encrusted with a range of gem-set cabochons and materials such as turquoise, lapis, agate, malachite, mother-of-pearl and blister pearl. Always of a refined and charming elegance, Cymric and Tudric wares are as eagerly sought on the market by today's Art Nouveau collector as they were at their debut.

144   It was Liberty's policy not to identify or acknowledge its designers, but the most talented of these are now known: Archibald Knox, Rex Silver, Oliver Baker, Cecil Aldin, Bernard Cuzner and a Miss Coggin. Knox was clearly the most important of them. Born on the Isle of Man, he developed a fanciful grammar of decorative ornament based on remote Celtic and Manx designs – mainly those from the 7th to 11th centuries – which he presumably studied on the island's crosses and grave memorials, and on its runic monument. Other stylistic influences evident in his work are The Book of Kells and the selection of complex interlacing motifs illustrated in Owen Jones's *The Grammar of Ornament*, first published in 1856.

The majority of Liberty's metalwares were manufactured by William H. Haseler of Birmingham, whose production included a wide range of gold and silver wares, as well as jewelry, for other retailers. Haseler also supplied the Tudric pewter mounts for the glass

174

jugs and decanters commissioned by Liberty from James Powell & Sons, of Whitefriars.

Apart from Hasler, Birmingham was a major centre at the turn of the century for silver production and study. The city's Central School of Art and Victoria Street School for Jewellers and Silversmiths offered progressive technical and design instruction, following which graduates could proceed to its Guild of Handicraft, for whom Arthur Dixon served as an important silver designer. Beyond Birmingham, a number of manufacturers generated Art Nouveau silver similar to that of Haseler – James Dixon & Sons, Mappin & Webb, and William Hutton & Sons, all of Sheffield; and the Silver Studio, owned by Arthur Silver and then his son, Reginald (Rex), Connell, and Wakely & Wheeler, in and around London.

Also in London, several individual silversmiths and designers applied their talents intermittently to the new modernism, mostly as only one strand in a diverse repertory. Omar Ramsden, in partnership with the designer Alwyn C.E. Carr, produced a medieval type of silverware remarkable for its rich forms and imagery; the signature *Ramsden me fecit* survives as a delightful reminder of the widespread preoccupation with neo-classicism in the late 1800s. Alexander Fisher 145

145 Alexander Fisher, silver jug, 1905

146 C.R. Ashbee, table lamp, silver base set with amethysts, 1900

was another traditionalist, who, although trained as a sculptor, made his reputation as an enamellist. The well-known designer-architect C.R. Ashbee also turned his hand on occasion to the field of silver, 146 drawing on both old and new imagery; in one instance, he used 17th-century rat-tail spoon motifs, and in another, curvilinear whiplash elements fresh from the Continent. Others associated with silver work of the period were Gilbert Leigh Mark, who had a predilection for embossed motifs suggestive of plant forms, and Nelson Dawson, the founder in 1901 of the Artificers' Guild, who had been trained in enamels by Fisher. Most of these had their silver designs executed by guild artisans, whose own Art Nouveau silverware creations were characterized by the liberal use of vibrant enamels and a robust style of chasing and finishing in which the burin and hammer marks were left visible on the silver's surface to emphasize its handcraftsmanship.

Christopher Dresser designed household appliances in the late 1800s which prefigured the 20th-century modern movement – not Art Nouveau, whose stylizations it bypassed, but rather Cubism and the functionalism of the 1920s and '30s. Dresser produced a wide gamut of unadorned industrial objects, their forms based on the lozenge, cube, triangle and sphere, for silver and silver-plate manufacturers such as J.W. Hukin & J.T. Heath and F. Elkington, of Birmingham, and James Dixon & Sons of Sheffield. Even today, his designs retain an astonishing modernity in their crisp purity of form.

The 1871 proclamation of the King of Prussia as German Emperor unified that country's numerous principalities and led to its rapid industrialization. Economic growth brought prosperity and with it a burgeoning bourgeoisie who sought precious objects as a measure of their elevated status within society. The majority of the silver and metalware produced in Germany during this period was traditional – particularly *Altdeutsche Stil* (Renaissance style) and neo-Rococo – but the metalware industry did respond hesitantly around 1900 to *Jugendstil*. This fell broadly into three categories: a floral vernacular of ornament inspired by the French interpretation of the new art; an asymmetrical curvilinear one based on the Brussels School (especially van de Velde and Horta); and a more severe geometrical style that echoed that of the Vienna Secessionists. In Munich, the Vereinigte Werkstätten für Kunst im Handwerk, founded in 1897, created a highly distinctive modernist style in which scrolled floral ornament, piercing and bosses predominated.

Metalware production in Germany in this period was concentrated around Berlin, Darmstadt, Dresden, Hagen (on the Ruhr) and, as

147 Hugo Leven, for J.P. Kayser und Söhne, pewter water sprinkler, *c.* 1898

noted, Munich. Manufacturers outside these centres included P. Bruckmann und Söhne in Heilbronn; Koch und Bergfeld and Wilkens und Söhne in Bremen; and the Württembergische Metallwaren Fabrik (WMF) in Geislingen. Individual artist-craftsmen and designers likewise turned their hand to *Jugendstil* silver: in Darmstadt, Ernst Riegel and his successor Theodor Wende, Peter Behrens, Hans Christiansen and Patriz Huber; in Weimar, van de Velde; and in Berlin, Emile Lettre.

In addition to the production of silver, several German factories applied a charming range of floral and curvilinear *Jugendstil* motifs to pewterware. Notable in this category were Walter Scherf & Co., which marketed its wares under the trade name 'Osiris', and Orion Zinn, in Nuremberg; J.P. Kayser und Söhne in Krefeld; and Orivit

148 Württembergische Metallwaren Fabrik (WMF), ladle, silver plated metal, and
punch bowl, silver plated metal and glass, *c.* 1900

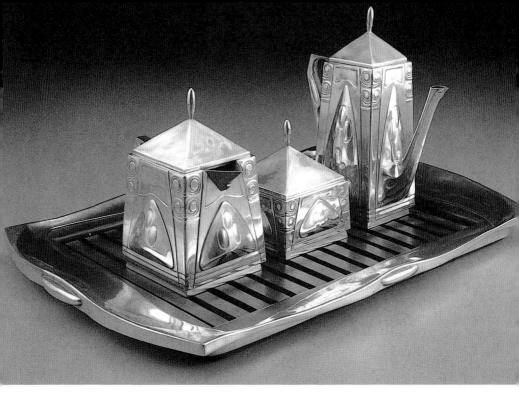

149 Josef M. Olbrich, tea and coffee service, pewter and teak, *c.* 1904

AG in Cologne-Braunsfeld. *Jugendstil* domestic wares by these firms – for example, claret and water jugs, tea caddies, beakers and candlesticks – are today avidly sought by collectors of Art Nouveau metalware.

149 It is now often difficult to identify the individual metalware designers and craftsmen who participated in the Austrian Secessionist movement; most were associated between 1900 and 1914 with either the Kunstgewerbeschule or the Wiener Werkstätte, or more frequently with both. Whereas Hoffmann and Moser dominated the designs for items such as flower baskets, light fixtures and tazzas, there were others, such as Czeschka and Peche, who contributed significantly to the highly distinctive and attractive Austrian modernist look with a similar range of fluted and pierced table-top wares.

Belgium's contribution to the field of Art Nouveau silverware was small, but of the highest calibre. Van de Velde showed his easy facility with the medium in a number of characteristic abstract curvilinear designs for household accessories executed both in Germany and in his workshops in Ixelles, a Brussels suburb. Wolfers, too, introduced silver into a number of his *tours de force*, including tablewares and a crystal vase with a sumptuous peacock silver mount – as did Frans Hoosemans, whose silver-and-ivory studies of nudes posing among slender flowers, done in collaboration with the sculptor Egide Rombaux, were fashioned into candelabra that have come to personify the Art Nouveau figural creation at its highest level of sensitivity. Fernand Dubois also chose silver for a pair of candelabra comprised of entwined stalks that pulsate with motion.

In Holland, the modernist art vocabulary was broadly rejected in favour of geometric patterns evocative of antiquity, especially those of pharaonic Egypt and the Levant. Those factories and individual designers who did respond to the Art Nouveau movement, such as the firm of J.M. van Kempen in Voorschoten, and Professor A.F. Gips, did so with a floral interpretation. Gips's silver designs were executed by the firm of C.J. Begeer of Utrecht.

Around 1900, the Scandinavian countries drew on national folklore for their decorative inspiration, especially in Norway, where Viking-revival imagery enjoyed great popularity. Another characteristic of Norwegian silver at the time was its use of enamel as a means of embellishment. At least two designers in Christiania (now Oslo), Gustav Gaudernack and Thorolf Prytz, created Art Nouveau flower-form silverware with *plique-à-jour* petals and leaves in a style reminiscent of Feuillâtre. The Christiania silversmiths J. Tostrup and David-Andersen executed works of this high technical calibre.

Danish Art Nouveau silver was dominated by George Jensen, who trained in the Copenhagen workshop of Mogens Ballin, in his own right an accomplished metalworker whose wares were offered through the gallery La Maison Moderne in Paris. Jensen made his first silverware and jewelry while in Mogens Ballin's employment, around 1901. In 1904 he opened his own workshop, where at first he produced only jewelry. Flat- and hollow-ware designs followed after a while. These were mostly devoid of ornament; the material's fluid contours and planished surfaces were considered decoration enough. Soon, however, Jensen abandoned such simplicity for organic forms of ornamentation, such as bouquets of flowers and bunches of fruit, with which he adorned the finials, openwork bases and handles on his vessels and cutlery. Always of an irreproachable harmony and logic, Jensen's designs soon reached an eager international market. His best-

150

known patterns, such as the 'Konge' (Acorn), are today still in production, and have a timeless, lyrical quality that transcends the cycles that dictate the fashions of the moment. Jensen was assisted through the years by a number of outstanding designers, of whom Johan Rohde and Harald Nielsen are especially well-known.

In the United States, the large silver factories and retailers were unpersuaded by the advent of Art Nouveau, in large part because their main clients were wealthy patrician families in whom they had instilled the belief that traditional European-style silverware alone would provide the true measure of social refinement and respectability. They therefore distanced themselves from the new movement, which flaunted itself as anti-establishment. On those occasions when the more prestigious silvermakers, such as Tiffany & Company and Black, Starr & Frost in New York, and Bailey, Banks & Biddle in Philadelphia, did introduce variety into their repertory towards the end of the century, they opted for a charming selection of *Japoniste* metalwares rendered in silver with copper encrustations or with

150 George Jensen, pair of silver grape-pattern candelabra, 1920

151 Gorham Company, *Morning and Night*, pair of candelabra, silver, made for the St Louis Exhibition, 1904

minute *niello* detailing. A notable exception was the Gorham   151
Company of Providence, which introduced an exuberant series of Art
Nouveau silverware, named *Martele*, that was adorned with highly
embossed floral and vegetal motifs. *Martele* silver contained a higher
silver content (.95) than the firm's standard wares (.925).

Other prominent American silver makers, such as the Alvin
Manufacturing Company and Theodore B. Starr in New York, Reed
and Barton in Taunton, Mass., and J. E. Caldwell and Simon Bros. in
Philadelphia, responded to the new art with a series of floral patterns,
such as primrose, orchids and azalea, that were reserved for a small
number of their hollow- and flat-ware services.

Only one company, Unger Brothers of Newark, N.J., attempted
to recreate faithfully the ostentatious *femme-fleur* imagery of the Paris
Salons, which it did on a broad range of stamped toiletry items and
jewelry. Languorous Belle Epoque maidens reclined on or clambered
over handmirrors, powder boxes, belt buckles and brooches in such

profusion that around 1905 they slipped into *kitsch* as readily as did their French counterparts. William B. Kerr, a Newark neighbour, produced a similar line of high-style wares, in which nymphs disported themselves amid foliage.

Small American metal studios and individual metalworkers were more easily drawn to Art Nouveau's floral decorative vernacular than the large factories were. Most, however, preferred a realistic interpretation to the modish stylizations on the Continent. In addition, particular emphasis was given by the individual artisan to handcraftsmanship – to the extent that such works are today defined rather as 'Arts and Crafts' than as 'Art Nouveau'. Notable works in silver and other metals in this category were created by the Kalo Shops, Lebolt & Company and Robert Jarvie in Chicago; Shreve & Company in San Francisco; and Elizabeth Copeland in Boston.

CHAPTER NINE

Sculpture

In the 19th century, the phases in the development of French sculpture corresponded broadly to the two main divisions in the nation's political history: the reign of Louis-Philippe from 1830 to 1848 and the Second Empire from 1851 to 1870. It was only with the formation of the Third Empire following the 1870 Commune that sculpture, like painting, could start to rid itself of the debilitating influence of the State.

Prior to 1870 the road to sculptural acclaim had been as clearly marked as it had been narrow. All but a small percentage of French sculptors studied at the Ecole des Beaux-Arts in Paris. There, year after stultifying year, the students competed for the top academic honour, the Prix de Rome, a distinction awarded to those who best interpreted the limited classical idiom of their professors, who had themselves passed through the same educational process a generation or two earlier. Over all those who defied the system, the tyranny continued whether they were Beaux-Arts trained or not. David d'Angers and François Rude, for example, were forced into exile on the coup d'état of Louis-Napoléon in 1851.

In addition, the only means of reaching the public was by exhibiting at the annual Salons, the entries for which were judged by members of the 'Institut', and, naturally enough, any sculpture that failed to conform to its autocratic standards was rejected. André Précault was totally banned from the Salons from 1834 to 1848, and the works of Barye, Daumier and Fratin were refused repeatedly. Traditionalism was *de rigueur*, all the more so as the State was for many years almost the sole patron in its commissioning of monumental statuary that Baudelaire described pertinently as 'heroic didacticism'. As late as 1895, Frédéric Auguste Bartholdi's prize-winning entry at the Salon was his patriotic, but absurdly titled allegorical group, *Switzerland Comforting the Anguish of Strasbourg during the Siege of 1870*. Bartholdi's reputation is far more secure resting on his *Statue of Liberty* in New York harbour.

Parallel to the government's patronage of public monuments, however, was the gradual demand throughout the century for private ownership of sculpture as *objets d'art* for home ornamentation. The commercial opportunities afforded by the expanding buying power of the bourgeoisie were first anticipated by Ferdinand Barbedienne who, on opening his foundry in 1838, promptly used the invention of his friend and partner Achille Collas, which was described in an 1859 obituary in *La Gazette des Beaux-Arts* as 'the springboard to the uplifting of the masses'. Called a pantograph, it operated on a principle of fixed mathematical proportion. A tracing needle moved over the surface of a model (usually plaster or bronze) that was attached by a linkage system to a cutting stylus that reproduced the model on a reduced scale as a soft plaster blank. In a complex model, individual parts could be reduced separately and later joined. The pantograph allowed for the accurate reduction of bronze statues for reproduction in bronze, and harvested not only a large number of *bronzes d'édition* but also handsome profits for Barbedienne, who drew on all eras of Classical statuary for the subject-matter of these limited editions. Favourites were works by Giovanni Bologna and Andrea Riccio, but Barbedienne also catered to the growing demand for Romantic sculpture. In this way he provided a forum around 1900 for the promotion of sculpture outside of the Salon.

Other foundries and editing houses followed suit in the production of serialized bronzes for the mass market. In Paris, for example, E. Colin, Susse *frères*, Louchet and Thiébaut *frères* were active from the mid-1800s, and they were joined during the century's closing years by Hébrard, Houdebine, Valsuani and Siot-Decauville. These firms either negotiated copyrights with prominent sculptors such as Carrier-Belleuse and Carpeaux to reproduce in metal a variety of their works or, alternatively, commissioned them to create wax, clay or plaster maquettes of specific objects for subsequent reduction and conversion into metal.

By the 1890s the revolution sparked by the Communards twenty years earlier had likewise begun to drive the *ancien régime* out of the Salons. No longer was sculpture of a preordained style, size or subject-matter. Now it allied itself, on the one hand, with the Art Nouveau philosophy of integrated wholes and, on the other, with the concept of 'l'art dans tout' – that all household objects, whatever their function, should be aesthetic. Sculpture was therefore adapted into chimney-mantel garnitures, ashtrays, centrepieces, firedogs and light fixtures. These had previously been considered beneath the *métier*,

152 Jean-Auguste Dampt, *La Fée Mélusine et le Chevalier Raymondin*, steel ivory and precious jewels, 1894

particularly since these objects were not intended as unique pieces but as models for serialized editions. Now, however, celebrated sculptors such as Raoul Larche, Théodore Rivière, Pierre Roche and Maurice Bouval could depend less, if they wished, on the commissions for unique pieces than on the royalties that accrued from the mass production of their works. (It is understandable that at a time when Rodin was being hailed as the new Phidias, many of his contemporaries felt the need *not* to compete and were therefore prepared to reduce the scale of their sculpture.)

The preferred sculptural materials at the turn of the century were marble, stone, terracotta and bronze. Mixed-media groups and statuettes were also exhibited by such sculptors as Jean Dampt, Georges Lemaire and Louis-Ernest Barrias. Ivory came back into

152

vogue following the Belgian colonization of the Congo by King Leopold and the Terveuren exhibition of 1897.

It was bronze that emerged as the unquestioned favourite, largely because of the Collas machine. Art Nouveau bronzes, however, were not cheap, and as a result editions also appeared in alloys or fashioned by an electro-typing process patented by Christofle. This process made it possible to use less expensive base metals, such as zinc, which were electroplated with a more expensive metal, such as silver or gold.

For their inspiration, Art Nouveau sculptors drew on the same range of themes we have seen in the other disciplines of the decorative arts. The botanical and entomological motifs on Gallé's cameo lampshades and on Lalique's jewelry were portrayed on sculptural objects as well. The insect demi-monde of the praying mantis, cicada and stag beetle swarmed and crawled across inkwells, *épergnes* and vases that had cunningly been disguised as convolvuli and waterlilies. Whiplash and scrolled designs – reaching their apogee in the cast and wrought openwork balustrades of Victor Horta and in the writhing extravagances of Hector Guimard's Métro entrances – were also in the vocabulary of sculpture. All the period's most recognizable themes – and clichés – were, in fact, used, although none more exhaustively than 'Woman'. Her domination of the decorative arts of the 1900s, and of sculpture in particular, was extraordinary. Representative of all that the Belle Epoque and 'les années insouciantes' stood for (so erroneously), women appeared on almost everything in low, high or full relief. Freed from the real-life metal and whalebone harnesses into which fashion had locked them, and freed also from their equally stifling respectability (so aptly portrayed in the novels of Stendhal, Balzac and Flaubert), women threw caution, clothes and corsets to the winds. This, at least, was how Art Nouveau sculptors depicted them, an interpretation that the critics at the Salons tended to endorse in their reviews. Interpreted as nymphs, naiads or undines, who were variously melancholy, ethereal or somnambulistic, the maidens who adorned sculpture around 1900 had their antecedents in the Symbolist movement that had pervaded the worlds of both literature and painting twenty years earlier.

The Symbolists were originally inspired by the English Aesthetic Movement and by the Pre-Raphaelites. Their distaste for realism could be found in the Baudelairean ideal, 'Sois belle et sois triste' (Be beautiful and sad), and in Rossetti's *Beatrice*. Courbet's models, who had never been troubled by so much as the shadow of a thought, no

188

longer offered sufficient intellectual inspiration. The women now painted by Gustave Moreau, Pierre Puvis de Chavannes, Fernand Khnopff and Odilon Redon incorporated a blend of the satanic, erotic, spiritualistic and funereal. Philippe Julian, in his *Dreamers of Decadence*, described the new 'Belle Dame sans Merci':

> Princess or artist's model, sphinx or succubus, Sappho or Ganymede, the *fin-de-siècle* insisted that the face should be moulded by the soul, and this was the mask which obtained the greatest success. In order to be desirable in a milieu which had turned its back on materialism, woman had to become a lily if she did not want to be condemned as vulgar by the Aesthetes. If woman could not be childlike and innocent, she was expected to inspire evil desires.

And this she did. With her enigmatic expression and eyes closed to conceal an inner world of reveries, the Symbolist woman conjured up images of death-ridden chimeras, sorcery and the current cult for hallucinatory drug-taking.

The Art Nouveau woman, in turn, represented an offshoot of this theme, albeit a rather effete one. Gone was the *femme fatale*; in her place a tousled enchantress. Woman's new role was allegorical. Though still symbolic, she now personified such ideals as Justice, Faith, Truth and Progress; and in the guise of Progress she would be shown brandishing aloft a torch, and became the Fairy Electricity. Thus she symbolized the invention of the incandescent filament bulb and, by projection, the triumph of Science over Mechanics, and indeed the new century over the old.

Nobody personified the electric light in sculpture more than the American dancer, Loïe Fuller. Arriving in Paris in 1892, she established herself at the Folies Bergère where the uniqueness of her various illuminated dances led to immediate and spectacular success. Isadora Duncan, at first a protégée of Miss Fuller, described Fuller's impact on the audience in her autobiography, *My Life*:

> Before our very eyes she turned to many-colored shining orchids, to a wavering flowing sea-flower and at length to a spiral-like lily, all magic of Merlin, the sorcery of light, color, flowing form. What an extraordinary genius . . . she was one of the first original inspirations of light and changing color – she became light.

The electric light was still, of course, a curiosity and this made Loïe the inspiration for numerous sculptors, who sought to convey the magic

154 Alphonse Mucha, bust, probably for the Fouquet showroom, gilt-bronze, silver and marble, *c.* 1900

155 Raoul Larche, figural lamp of Loïe Fuller, gilt-bronze, *c.* 1900

156 Raoul Larche, inkwell, gilt-bronze, c. 1902

of her performances in metal. The most notable of these was Raoul
Larche, who had been a student of Alexandre Falguière and Eugène 155
Delaplanche at the Ecole des Beaux-Arts in Paris before making his
debut in 1881 at the Salon of the Soçiété des Artistes Français.

An undated catalogue in the library of the Musée des Arts
Décoratifs in Paris of a posthumous exhibition of Larche's works is the
major key to the extent of his life's work – a life tragically cut short in
1912 when he was run down by an automobile. The exhibition
displayed hundreds of Larche's paintings and sculpture, the latter as
varied in its subject-matter as it was diverse in its materials. Busts of
mythological deities, groups of peasant girls, figurines of sword-
bearing youths and of naiads clasping conch and triton shells were
executed in a dazzling array of stone, white biscuit porcelain, pewter,
bronze and terracotta. To these were added a range of heavily

157 Louis Chalon, dish, bronze, c. 1903

156 accented Art Nouveau bronze objects: busts, table lamps, inkwells and cache-pots.

157   Another prominent sculptor at the turn of the century was Louis Chalon. Initially a painter, he became an accomplished illustrator, gem-setter and couturier of royal capes. His entry into the field of sculpture in 1898 was fortuitous: on being asked to design a series of *trompe-l'oeil* illustrations intended to provide the impression of white-and-blue porcelain, he decided, after several unsatisfactory attempts, to model them first in painted wax. The resulting effect was so charming that further models for other objects followed, and these, in turn, became the maquettes for an extensive range of bronzes cast by

160 the founder Louchet. Chalon had a penchant for the woman-flower hybrid; nubile maidens gambol on his vases, garniture mantel sets, sweetmeat boxes and centrepieces. His design of the *Vase of the Hesperides*, which he displayed at the 1900 Exposition Universelle, was executed for him by the ceramist Emile Muller. The vase stood 7 feet high and depicted the three daughters of Atlas supporting the sea monsters who guarded the garden of the Hesperides.

194

Léo Laporte-Blairsy, born in Toulouse, received his art training, 158 like so many of his contemporaries, from the grandmaster Falguière, before making his debut at the Salons in 1887. Starting out as a sculptor and engraver of rather large monuments and busts, he decided in the late 1890s that he would reduce the scale of his work to meet the increasing demand for household *objets d'art*. His main area of concentration was sculptural lamps. His themes, described in 1903 by the critic de Félice as 'luminous fantasies', represented a strange mixture of the anecdotal, the eclectic and Art Nouveau. Some, such as his table lamp *La Fillette au ballon*, which depicts a young girl holding up a balloon she has just bought at the Magasins du Louvre, tell a story. Others, fashioned either as Breton women or Greek dancers, are inspired by history. He was also capable of pure 1900 Art Nouveau creations, such as his umbel and peacock table lamps.

Maurice Bouval exhibited his work through the Salon of the 159 Soçiété des Artistes Français and the Maison Goldscheider. His bronzes combined sensual nymphs, waterlilies, lotus blossoms and

158 Léo Laporte-Blairsy, two figural lamps, bronze, *c.* 1902

159 Maurice Bouval, *Obsession* and *Dream*, pair of candelabra, silver, 1900

poppies with a sometimes strong suggestion of symbolism and the supernatural. In the heavy-lidded eyes of his *Orphélia* bust, the mystique of his *Le Secret* statuette (no doubt inspired by Pierre Fix-Masseau's on the same theme several years earlier), and the trance-like state of the maidens in his *Dream* and *Obsession* candelabra, there is something of the phantasmagoria of Poe and the 1890s Parisian rage for the *heure de la verte* (absinthe-drinking time).

161   Joseph Chéret was a sculptor who, following tutelage under Vallois and Carrier-Belleuse (Chéret later married the latter's daughter), made his Salon debut in 1863. In 1887 he succeeded to the directorship of the modelling studio at the Manufactory of Sèvres. Chéret died in 1894, before Art Nouveau had become firmly established, but his style anticipated the movement's high point, which came fully ten

196

160 Charles Louchet and Lamarre, ceramic vase
with enamelled gilt-bronze mount, 1898

161 Joseph Chéret, wall
bracket for his founder
Soleau, 1900

162 Charles Korschann, gilt-
bronze table lamp with
inkwell, c. 1902

years after his death. Chéret's designs for bronzes were executed by
the Parisian founder Soleau and would normally, on his death, have
ceased to be reproduced. His style, though for the most part Second
Empire, was occasionally transitional – part Classical and part Art
Nouveau. Gilt-bronze putti either romp among irises and waterlilies
(the corolla of which sometimes housed electric bulbs), or attention is
lavished on some of the earliest *fin-de-siècle* maidens. Soleau was quick
to appreciate, after 1894, that Chéret's theme was increasingly in
vogue, and he therefore had several of the original bronzes re-cast
from Chéret's models still in his studio. These editions were
introduced in 1900 and 1904.

162   Active in Paris between 1894 and 1906, Charles Korschann, a
sculptor and medallist, was born in Brno, Moravia, and graduated
from both the Viennese and Berlin Schools of Fine Arts. He led a
maverick life, with sojourns in Paris, Berlin, Frankfurt, Cracow and
again in Brno. It was during his stay in Paris that he designed a series of
Art Nouveau small objects, such as clocks, inkwells and portrait busts.

163 Agathon Léonard, two gilt-bronze lamps in the form of dancers, from his *Jeu de l'écharpe* series, *c.* 1903

In 1904, for example, he was commissioned by the Moravian Museum in Brno to do a bust of Alphonse Mucha.

A generation older than most of those who applied their talents to the Art Nouveau movement, Jean-Auguste Dampt had already, by 1876, attended both Ecoles des Beaux-Arts in Dijon and Paris, and made his debut at the Salons. Primarily a sculptor, he switched readily from marble to stone, wood and ivory, to emerge as one of the period's most versatile mixed-media exponents. He exhibited such objects as furniture, sculpture and light fixtures through the Soçiété Nationale des Beaux-Arts and the exhibitions of 'L'Art dans Tout', a group of six avant-garde artists who chose to exhibit outside the formality of the annual Salons. Dampt is remembered for his superlative *La Fée Mélusine et le Chevalier Raymondin* group in 1894 of 152 a knight in steel armour kissing a jewel-encrusted ivory maiden, and for his wood-and-ivory *Paix du Foyer* statuette four years later.

Agathon Léonard (real name Léonard-Agathon van Weydeveld) was born of Belgian parents in Lille, where he attended the Academy of Fine Arts. Settling in Paris, he designed and executed portrait busts, groups and statuettes in rose quartz, green Egyptian marble, *flambé* earthenware, bronze, ivory and plaster. In 1902 he exhibited two particularly fine busts in rose quartz at the Salon, *Mélancolie* and *Méditation*. Léonard is now known almost exclusively for his *Jeu de l'Echarpe* (scarf game) series of coryphee figurines. These were first 163 displayed in 1897 as 'a project for the decoration of the foyer of a dance hall'. Later, the Manufactory of Sèvres commissioned Léonard to model the series in white biscuit porcelain for its pavilion at the 1900 Exposition Universelle. Pieces could be purchased either as the complete set or individually, and so successful was the project that the founders, Susse *frères*, subsequently bought the right to have the originals cast in gilt-bronze.

On leafing through the catalogues of the annual Paris Salons between 1895 and 1914, one sees how many sculptors there were, and why there is still today a substantial supply of objects to be found from that epoch in flea markets, antique shops and auctions. Statuettes were made by Lucien Alliot, Max Blondat and Julien Caussé; groups by 166 Félix and Alexandre Charpentier; candlesticks and plaques by Georges Flamand, Charles Jonchery and Auguste Ledru; sculptural 153,165,164

164 Auguste Ledru, tobacco jar, bronze *c.* 1902

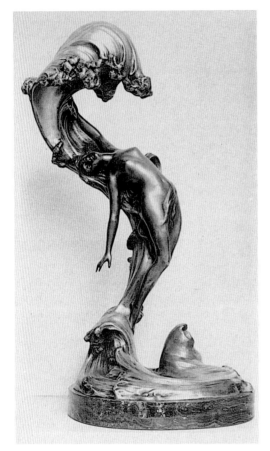

165 Charles Jonchery, figural lamp, c. 1901

166 Max Blondat, clock, c. 1901

lamps by five of the Moreau family; and portrait busts by Théodore
167 Rivière, Pierre Roche, Villé Vallgren and Emmanuel Villanis. Many,
many more were at work at the time, attempting to satisfy what
appears to have been a gluttonous market.

Beyond Paris, Art Nouveau sculpture was found less frequently. In
168 Austria, Gustav Gurschner displayed his work through the Viennese
Secession group from 1898, later participating in numerous exhibitions in Munich, Paris and Monte Carlo. His reputation grew
accordingly. In the early part of his career he devoted himself to
monumental groups and portrait busts, but then, like Laporte-

202

167 Emmanuel Villanis, bronze bust, *La Fiancée*, c. 1900

168 Gustav Gurschner, bronze and
Turbo Marmoratus shell table
lamp, *c.* 1901

169 Philippe Wolfers, marble and
enamelled bronze lamp called *La
Fée au Paon* (Peacock Fairy), *c.* 1900

Blairsy, he turned his hand to smaller household objects such as door-knockers, lady's hand mirrors, pen trays and lamps. Gurschner's metalwork shows great refinement. Even his use of bare-breasted young women – potentially such a hackneyed theme – as the central figures in many of his objects largely survives any stricture for they have a quiet dignity and poetic charm and are never vulgar. A favourite Gurschner practice was to use sea-shells – for example, the chambered nautilus and the Turbo Marmoratus – to house the electric bulbs in his sculptural lamps. The shells' natural translucency produced a richly luminescent effect when viewed by transmitted light.

In Brussels, Philippe Wolfers was apprenticed to his father's studio in 1876 before studying under Isidore de Rudder as a sculptor. It was only after the Terveuren exhibition in 1897, in which he showed such works as his *Fée au paon* and *Caresse de cygne*, however, that Wolfers began to concentrate on jewelry, for which he is today more celebrated. His *Fée au paon* statue is one of the period's masterpieces. It consists of a life-size marble nude holding a bronze peacock. Electric bulbs are positioned in the peacock's tail, the light rays being

169

170 Egide Rombaux and Frans Hoosemans, silver and ivory candelabrum, *c.* 1900

transmitted through *plique-à-jour* enamel 'eyes' set into the bronze. Wolfers displayed a similar group in ivory and bronze at the 1901 Salon of the Société Nationale des Beaux-Arts.

Also in Brussels, the sculptor and medallist Egide Rombaux worked with the silversmith Frans Hoosemans to produce a series of highly decorative candelabra and small table lamps. Hoosemans fashioned the silver tendrils and stems that enveloped Rombaux's sculpted ivory maidens to culminate in flower-form candle-nozzles or bulb-holders.

Art Nouveau sculpture carried the seeds of its own downfall. Woman was exploited *ad nauseam*, and the public's appetite was soon satiated.

170

206

Bibliography

Sources of Illustrations

Index

Bibliography

General

Amaya, Mario *Art Nouveau* London/ New York 1966
Art Nouveau, Art and Design at the Turn of the Century (Metropolitan Museum of Art) New York 1935
Aslin, Elizabeth *The Aesthetic Movement: Prelude to Art Nouveau* London 1969
Barilli, Renato *Art Nouveau* London 1966
Battersby, Martin *The World of Art Nouveau* New York/London 1968
Benton, T. and Millikin, S. *Art Nouveau 1890–1902* Milton Keynes 1975
Charpentier, Françoise-Thérèse *Art Nouveau, L'Ecole de Nancy* Paris 1987
Garner, Philippe *The Encyclopedia of Decorative Arts* London 1978
Geffroy, G. *Les Industries artistiques françaises et étrangères à l'exposition universelle de 1900* Paris 1900
Johnson, Diane Chalmers *American Art Nouveau* New York 1979
Jullian, Philippe *The Triumph of Art Nouveau, Paris Exhibition 1900* New York 1974
Klopp, Gerard (ed.) *Nancy 1900, Rayonnement de l'art nouveau* Thionville 1989
Larner, Gerald and Celia *The Glasgow Style* New York 1979
Madsen, Stephen Tschudi *Sources of Art Nouveau* Oslo 1956
Pevsner, Nikolaus *Pioneers of the Modern Movement from William Morris to Walter Gropius* London 1936
Powell, Nicholas *The Sacred Spring: The Arts in Vienna 1898–1918* London 1974
Rheims, Maurice *L'Objet 1900* Paris 1964
—*L'Art 1900* Paris 1965
Schmutzler, Robert *Art Nouveau* London/New York 1967 (pb 1979)
Schorske, Carl E. *Fin-de-Siècle Vienna* New York/ London 1979
Selz Peter (The Museum of Modern Art) *Art Nouveau* New York 1960
Stoddard, William O. *The Story of America* New York 1955

Vergo, P. *Art in Vienna, 1898–1918* London 1975
Waissenberger, Robert (ed.) *Vienna 1890–1920* New York 1984
Weisberg, Gabriel P. *Art Nouveau Bing: Paris Style 1900* New York 1986
Wheeler, Candace *Principles of Decoration* New York 1903

Architecture

Benton, Tim and Charlotte (ed.) *Architecture and Design, 1890–1939: An International Anthology of Original Articles* New York 1975
Casteels, M. *The New Style: Architecture and Decorative Design* London 1931
Collins, G.R. *Antonio Gaudi* New York 1960
Curtis, William J.R. *Modern Architecture* Englewood Cliffs, N.J., 1982
Hitchcock, H.R. *Architecture: Nineteenth and Twentieth Centuries* Harmondsworth 1958
Jordy, William H. *American Buildings and Their Architects; Progressive and Academic Ideals at the Turn of the Twentieth Century* (vol. 3) New York 1972
Pevsner, Nikolaus *The Sources of Modern Architecture and Design* London/New York 1968 (repr. 1989)
Russell, Frank (ed.) *Art Nouveau Architecture* London 1979

Furniture

Alison, F. *Charles Rennie Mackintosh as a Designer of Chairs* London 1974
Bossaglia, R. *Le Mobilier Art Nouveau* Paris 1972
Duncan, Alastair *Art Nouveau Furniture* London/New York 1982
—*Louis Majorelle* London/New York 1992
Howarth, Thomas *Charles Rennie Mackintosh and the Modern Movement* London 1952
Lambert, Théodore *Meubles et ameublements de style moderne* Paris 1905–06
Macleod, Robert *Charles Rennie Mackintosh* Feltham 1968

Mannoni, E. *Meubles et ensembles style 1900* Paris 1968

Olmer, Pierre *La Renaissance de mobilier français 1890–1910* Paris 1927

Prouvé, M. *Victor Prouvé* Nancy 1958

Tierlink, Herman *Henry van de Velde* Brussels 1959

Graphics

Arwas, Victor *Belle Epoque: Posters and Graphics* London 1978

Duncan, Alastair and de Bartha, Georges *Art Nouveau and Art Deco Bookbinding* London/New York 1989

Millman, Ian *Georges de Feure: Maître du Symbolisme et de l'art nouveau* Paris 1992

Mucha, Jírí *Alphonse Maria Mucha: His Life and Art* New York 1989

Rennert, Jack *Posters of the Belle Epoque* New York 1990

Walters, T. *Art Nouveau Graphics* New York 1971

Glass and Ceramics

Amaya, Mario *Tiffany Glass* London/New York 1967

Arwas, Victor *Glass: Art Nouveau to Art Deco* London 1977

—*Tiffany* London/New York 1979

Bangert, Albrecht *Glass: Art Nouveau and Art Deco* London/New York 1979

Bloch-Dermant, Janine *L'Art de Verre en France, 1860–1914* Paris 1974

Blount, Bernice and Henry *French Cameo Glass* Des Moines 1968

Doat, Taxile *Ceramic Movement in Europe in 1900* New York 1903

Duncan, Alastair and de Bartha, Georges *Glass by Gallé* London/New York 1984

Duncan, Alastair/Eidelberg, Martin/Harris, Neil *Masterworks of Louis Comfort Tiffany* London/New York 1989

Fare, Michel *La céramique contemporaine* Paris 1953

Freeman, Larry *Iridescent Glass* New York n.d.

Garner, Philippe *Emile Gallé* New York 1976

—*Glass 1900: Gallé, Tiffany, Lalique* London/New York 1979

Grover, Ray and Lee *Art Glass Nouveau* Rutland, Vt. 1968

Hilschenz, Helga *Das Glas des Jugendstils* Duesseldorf 1973

Koch, Robert *Louis C. Tiffany – Rebel in Glass* New York 1964

—S. Bing *Artistic America, Tiffany Glass and Art Nouveau* Cambridge, Mass. 1970

Koch, Robert *Louis C. Tiffany's Glass, Bronzes, Lamps* New York 1971

McKean, Hugh *The "Lost" Treasures of Louis Comfort Tiffany* New York 1980

McKearin, George S. and Helen *American Glass* New York 1941

—*Two Hundred Years of American Blown Glass* New York 1950

Peck, Herbert *The Book of Rookwood Pottery* New York 1968

Pelichet, Edgar *La céramique de la Belle Epoque* Geneva 1970

—*La céramique art nouveau* Lausanne 1976

Revi, Albert Christian *American Art Nouveau Glass* New York 1968

Rosenthal, Léon *La Verrerie française depuis cinquante ans* Paris 1927

Sowers, Robert *The Lost Art* New York 1954

Uecker, Wolf *Art Nouveau and Art Deco Lamps and Candlesticks* London 1986

Van Tassel, Valentine *American Glass* New York n.d.

Jewelry

Barten, Sigrid *René Lalique: Schmuck und Objets d'art 1890–1910* Munich 1978

Becker, Vivienne *Art Nouveau Jewelry* London/New York 1985

—(ed.) *The Jewellery of René Lalique* (exhibition catalogue) London 1987

The Belle Epoque of French Jewellery 1850–1910 London 1991

Eidelberg, Martin E. *Colonna* (exhibition catalogue) Dayton, Ohio 1983

Gere, Charlotte *European and American Jewellery 1830–1914* London 1975

Hughes, Graham *Modern Jewellery* London 1967

Nadelhoffer, Hans *Cartier, Jewelers Extraordinary* London/New York 1984

Sataloff, Joseph *Art Nouveau Jewelry* Bryn Mawr, PA 1984

Vever, Henri *La Bijouterie française au XIXe Siècle* (3 vols) Paris 1906

Silver

Aldburgham, Alison *Liberty's: A Biography of a Shop* London 1975

Calloway, Stephen (ed.) *The House of Liberty* London/Boston 1992

Carpenter, Charles H., Jr. *Gorham Silver 1831–1981* New York 1982

Holland, Margaret *Silver: An Illustrated Guide to American and British Silver* New York 1973

Hughes, Graham *Modern Silver throughout the World 1880–1967* New York 1967

Levy, Mervyn *Liberty Style. The Classic Years: 1898–1910* New York 1986

Scheidig, Walther *Crafts of the Weimar Bauhaus* London 1967

Tilbrook, Adrian J. *The Designs of Archibald Knox for Liberty & Co.* London 1976

Sculpture

Dinglestedt, K. *Le Modern Style dans les arts appliqués* Paris 1959

Duncan, Alastair *Art Nouveau Sculpture* London 1978

—*Art Nouveau and Art Deco Lighting* London/New York 1978

Periodicals

L'Art Décoratif 1898–1908
Art et Décoration 1899–1904
Art et Industrie (Nancy) 1900–1909
Brush and Pencil 1900–1903
Bulletin des Sociétés artistiques de l'est 1900–1904
The Cabinet Maker and Art Furnisher 1900–1901
Dekorative Kunst 1898–1903
Duetsche Kunst und Dekoration 1901–1904
Die Kunst 1899–1902
Kunst und Kunsthandwerk 1900–1904
La Lorraine Artiste 1899–1903
Meubles et Décors 1966
La Revue d'art 1899–1900
Revue Lorraine Illustrée 1903–1906
The Studio 1895–1907

Exhibition Catalogues

L'Art de Vivre: Decorative Arts and Design in France 1789–1989 Cooper-Hewitt Museum, New York, 1989

Brunhammer, Yvonne *Art Nouveau* Rice University and Art Institute of Chicago, 1976

Champier, Victor *Les Industries d'art à l'Exposition Universelle de 1900*, Paris 1902

Champigneulle, B. *Daum, cent ans de verre and de cristal* Musée des Beaux Arts, Nancy, 1976

Charpentier, Françoise-Thérèse *Broderies et Tissus* Musée de l'Ecole de Nancy, 1980

—*Louis Hestaux, collaborateur de Gallé* Musée de l'Ecole de Nancy, 1982

Drexler, Arthur and Daniel, Greta *Introduction to Twentieth Century Design* The Museum of Modern Art, New York, 1959

Exposition de l'Alliance Provinciale des Industries d'Art, L'Ecole de Nancy Union Centrale des Arts Décoratifs, Paris, 1903

L'Exposition d'art décoratif, Ecole de Nancy Salle Poirel, Nancy, 1904

Exposition d'art décoratif de l'Ecole de Nancy Société des Amis des arts de Strasbourg, Palais de Rohan, 1908

Exposition d'art décoratif et industriel lorrain, Salle Poirel, Nancy, 1894

L'Exposition de l'Ecole de Nancy, Armand Guermet, Paris 1903

Japonisme: Japanese Influence on French Art 1854–1910, Cleveland Musuem of Art/Rutgers University Art Gallery/Walters Art Gallery, Cleveland, New Brunswick, Baltimore 1975

Lambert, Théodore *Meubles de style moderne Exposition Universelle de 1900* Charles Schmid, n.d.

Liberty's 1875–1975 Victoria and Albert Musuem, London, 1975

Wittamer, Yolande Oostens *La Belle Epoque – Belgian Posters* (Wittamer-DeCamps collection) New York, 1971

Sources of Illustrations

Amsterdam: Rijksmuseum Vincent van Gogh 5; Photo Annan, Glasgow 29; Photo Barsoti, Florence 28; Georges de Bartha, Geneva 78; Photo Tim Benton 15; Berlin: Kunstgewerbemuseum, Staatliche Museen Preussischer Kulturbesitz 170; Borsje Collection, Paris 35, 37; Christie's, London 117, 127; Christie's, New York 16, 51, 53, 150, 151, 160; Corning, New York: The Rockwell Museum 84; Darmstadt: Hessisches Landesmuseum Darmstadt 115, 120; Photo Fischer Fine Art Ltd, London 49; Glasgow: Hunterian Art Gallery, University of Glasgow, Mackintosh Collection 17; Hamburg: Museum für Kunst und Gewerbe 64; Photo Benno Keysselitz 46, 77; London: By courtesy of the Board of Trustees of the Victoria & Albert Musuem 1, 6, 103, 128; Macklowe Gallery, New York 34, 159, 168; Photo Félix Marcilhac 50; Photo Mas 30; Moscow: Pushkin Musuem 54; Munich: Staatsmuseum 14; Nancy: Musée de l'Ecole de Nancy 76; New York: Courtesy of Cooper-Hewitt, National Museum of Design, Smithsonian Institution 52; Metropolitan Museum of Art 82, (Gift of Sarah E. Hanley, 1946) 131; Photo Richard Nickel 31; Norwest Corporation,

Minneapolis 70, 101, 106, 133, 141, 147, 148, (Rorstrand Company Collection Museum) 99; Oslo: Nasjonalgalleriet 57; Otterlo: Rijksmuseum Kröller-Müller 56; Paris: Musée des Arts Décoratifs 22, 32, 113, 114, (photo Jean-Loup Charmet) 12, (photo L. Sully-Jaulmes) 87, 91; Pforzheim: Schmuckmuseum 124; Philadelphia Museum of Art, Gift of Mr and Mrs Thomas E. Shipley, Jr 110; Private Collection 75, 108, 109, 111, 112, 116, 122, 125, 126, 129, 130, 144, 146, 153, 162, 163, 169; Minna Rosenblatt, New York 79; Collection Joel Schur 68; Collection of Benedict Silverman 136, 137, 143; Sotheby's, London 155; Sotheby's, New York 80, 83, 102, 105, 167; Photo Dr Franz Stoedtner 26; Photo Studio Minders 25; Vienna: Österreichische Galerie 59; Virginia Museum of Arts 44, 45, 47, 48, 55, 72, 123, 149, 154; Walthamstow: William Morris Gallery 2; Washington, D.C.: Courtesy of the Freer Gallery of Art, Smithsonian Institution, 7, (National Gallery of Art, Rosenwald Collection) 3; Collection of Mr and Mrs Harvey Weinstein 85; Winter Park, Florida: The Morse Gallery of Art 107; Zürich: Photo Kunstgewerbemuseum 18.

Index

Page numbers in italics refer to illustrations